Full Court Press

Full Court Press

A Young Basketball
Prodigy's Journey

By Eric Price

For my mother, Sharelita Price Mooney, who is the epitome of resilience and never gave up on her children

Chapter One

My passion for basketball hit me hard and hit me early. I always had a ball in my hand, dribbling it to school, to the store, and almost anywhere I went. There were a lot of great players in my neighborhood, and I watched them, I copied them, and I mimicked them. I not only played the game, but I studied it.

Basketball shaped me and transformed me during my childhood and teen years. When I was 8 years old, I played in a "10 and Under" Boys & Girls Club basketball game, against kids almost two years older than me, and I scored 25 points. I was dominating on the court, and the adults in the gym noticed. People started to talk and suddenly the adults in the neighborhood knew what the kids had already known for some time: I was good at basketball. This status gave me self-confidence. I had a special thing going for me that other little kids didn't have. My peers looked up to me when it came time to play basketball. It helped me make friends, and people respected me. This confidence carried over to the classroom, because I always had something to look forward to and something to feel good about, so I could focus at school and do well.

The specialness of my basketball talent was important because I grew up in a rough neighborhood. Sursum Corda, near the Capitol in Washington, D.C. was swarming with drug dealers and was known as one of the most active and violent drug markets in the city. When people in my later life asked me, 'How rough was it?", I tell them that that we had four generous and kind nuns who lived in our housing project, running programs for kids and adults and dedicating their lives to helping us. One time, they went on vacation for a week. The gangstas in the neighborhood broke into their house and stole all their belongings. They set up a yard sale in the parking lot of Sursum Corda, selling the nun's personal items, including religious recordings and even their socks. The nuns gave up and moved out after that.

I tell them that another time, two assistant District Attorneys and a police officer came to the neighborhood to start an anti-gang unit, and they were fired on by multiple drug dealers in a coordinated effort. We had shootings and murders all the time, the worst of which was when a 14-year-old girl was executed after she witnessed one drug dealer kill another.

I felt safe in my neighborhood, yet I also feared for my life. It was complex. We always said, "bullets don't have a name on them," because you never know if you are going to get hit. I had times when I got closer to the bullets than I ever wanted to. The first time was when I was 7 years old.

I stepped out my front door, ready to hurry over to my friend Bernard's house to play video games. I saw three police cars with their lights on and several cops standing outside, looking at the house two doors down from mine. Sursum Corda units were small, town house style, and close together, so this front door was only about eighty yards away from me. I should have turned back and gone inside, but instead I paused, then continued to walk forward. Just then a man popped out of the house and starting firing on the police.

Crack! Crack! Crack! I saw the bullets hit the side of the police car, making several big holes. I looked at the shooter and saw a determined face, he was firing repeatedly and backing himself toward the alley where he could escape to freedom.

I dropped to the ground, just as I had been taught. I covered my ears and I squeezed my eyes shut. My heart was racing. I felt true fear. The police didn't fire back at the man, and I've always felt that they held their fire because of me. When the man ran off into the alley, they chased after him. The police said nothing to me. I stood up and continued to Bernard's house.

When you're raised in a place where you experience violence, you see adults abusing drugs, and you realize that some people see no way out, it really changes you. But basketball brought new people and experiences to my life. I had coaches who believed in me, who helped me, and showed me patience and kindness. Basketball brought me to new places around the country, as far as

Hawaii, California, and Texas, all before I was 16 years old. I saw how other people lived, and I came to realize that there was a positive and fascinating world out there and I was eager to leave Sursum Corda behind and be a part of it.

One thing I learned in life is to look for that person who will believe in you. It was a challenge to keep believing in myself sometimes, so if I had someone rooting me on and showing me the way, that would make all the difference. I saw so much havoc around me, and many of my peers' lives were changed by violence, addiction, incarceration, or by poverty and low expectations. I needed an adult to have my back, to tell me I could achieve, and then I knew I could make it to the next level. I learned this at some point during my childhood, and it is what carried me through my teen years.

When I was very little, there were also some adults who thought I was a bad kid. Ms. Alverta Munlin was one them. She was the boss of the neighborhood, a lady who really ran the show. Adults had respect for her, kids were scared of her, and even the drug dealers would slink away if they saw her coming. She was an elected official, and on the management board of Sursum Corda. She also ran an inexpensive summer camp for the Sursum Corda kids which took place right in the circle and playground in our neighborhood I went to the camp, but Ms. Alverta never allowed me to participate in any of her fun trips because of my behavior. I'll never forget that feeling of seeing the big yellow school bus pulling up to take kids to the Six Flags amusement park. Kids were screaming and jumping with excitement.

Ms. Alverta would look at me and say to my mom, "He can NOT go."

I was trouble back then and Ms. Alverta knew it.

When I was eight years old, a friend and I set a trash can on fire in the elementary school parking lot. The friend was named Kenny Man and his dad was a notorious drug dealer and murderer. He was a young father, only about 25 years old, and his son was already following his lead. Kenny and I were friends and he would entice me to do bad things. Sometimes I was the one egging Kenny on, or daring him to do something. It felt thrilling on the one hand, and sad on the other to do these things.

One time, we robbed a taxi driver with a cap gun. "Give us your money, man!" we yelled.

The taxi man gave us about $20 since he thought it was real gun. I remember the look of confusion and fear on his face. We also robbed the IGA supermarket. We just went in there with our toy guns, pointed them at people, and stole candy. The girls working at the registers weren't scared of us as much as they were shocked that we would do this at such a young age. Kenny was robbing for a living by the time he was 12, but I was done with him by then.

Luckily, basketball interceded in my life soon after my period of bad behavior.

When my mother found out that I was responsible for the fire in the parking lot, she was concerned.

"Do you like playing with fire?" she asked.

"No," I said, "I promise I won't do it again."

She struck a match and put it on my hand for two seconds. My mom, Sharelita Price, always did the best she could to get our attention and try to make a positive impression on us. In this case, it worked, since I never played with fire again.

I went to church on Sundays, every week, no matter what. We got dressed up and walked to Southern Baptist Church to listen to Reverend Charles Doom. It was an enthusiastic service, with Rev. Doom half singling and half preaching,

"Somebody needs you this morning," yelled the Reverend as members of the congregation began to feel the Holy Spirit and cry, jump from their seats and yell along with the preacher. "Somebody is burdened here today, oh, we call on you, Jesus, because we know there is no one else we can call on." The congregation was active, enthusiastic, and the music was powerful.

My grandmother, Geraldine Price, was very involved with the church and she comes from a long line of women who proudly brought their family together each Sunday. We usually walked to church together, with my grandmother and my grandfather,

James Price, leading the way. My mom Sharelita, and my five aunts and uncles, along with other friends or cousins. It was a warm group and Sundays were always special to me.

In my earliest years, I lived with my mom and my brother Earl in Temple Courts, a high-rise public housing project next to Sursum Corda. My grandparents had a small townhouse at Sursum Corda, and Earl and I spent most of our days there, with my grandparents watching us while my mother was at work. My grandmother was a Head Start preschool teacher and great with children. I loved my grandparents and they were an influential and positive part of my life.

My father, Early Risby, was in my life in the very early years and I have a few faint memories of him. I recall him ironing my clothes and showing interest in me. By the time I was five or six, he was in prison for drug distribution and I didn't see him again until I was an adult. I did spend some time with his mother, my Grandma Sadie. She lived nearby in Maryland and owned a hair salon and was very warm and affectionate toward me. She was big on family and maintaining a connection even though my father was in prison for so long.

My mom gave birth to my sister, Shanika, when I was five. Her father wasn't in our lives for very long. I was very sweet to my little sister and protective of her. Eventually, she got into basketball too and that was something we connected over.

My brother Earl was named after our father, and he was a big part of my life. We are only a year and a half apart, so we were peers, friends, and rivals. He was confident and outgoing as a child, and I copied things that he did. I followed him around, and our mom would call after Earl, "Wait for your brother!"

People at Sursum Corda got used to seeing us as a pair. And in fact, many of our friends were pairs of brothers too, like Reggie and Paul Murray, and Michael and Tim Tyler. These were street guys who got into the drug trade early. When we were young kids, they wanted to hang out with the drug dealers and emulate them. We used to get in fights because they wanted to challenge me and Earl. We had to fight them off to prove ourselves. Especially later, when we were known as the athletes of Sursum Corda, other guys would challenge us. We had to let them know that we are from the same hood, we have the same instincts you have, so don't think that just because we are athletes and are trying to do something good, that we are soft.

Reggie died of an alcohol poisoning incident at sixteen and Paul started serving a long prison sentence in his late teens. A lot of the kids I played with as a child didn't make it to a happy and prosperous adulthood, unfortunately.

The other big landmark in my neighborhood and in my childhood was the Metropolitan Police Boys & Girls Club, #2. We called it "the club" or, if we were out in the city competing against other clubs, we called it

"#2". The Club was a haven for all the kids in the neighborhood. It wasn't safe to hang out in the horseshoe or the pathways and walkways through Sursum Corda where the drug trade was so vibrant. The Club was not only a hangout place for the kids, it also sponsored football, basketball and cheerleading teams, offered computer classes, homework help and field trips. A typical day for a Sursum Corda kid was to go to school, then right to the Club, and then home for dinner.

The reason that Sursum Corda was such a gold mine for the drug trade was because of its construction and its location. It was a six-acre plot of land off North Capitol Street, a short walk from Union Station, and not far from the Capitol building itself. It was close to the highways that took you to Maryland and Virginia, so it was easy for customers of the drug trade to drive into the horseshoe, make a purchase and then disappear into anonymity. It was also as if the design of the housing project was made especially for helping drug dealers to move their product and hide from police.

The architects of Sursum Corda were people who reacted to the impersonal high-rise housing projects of the past. Rather than having tall buildings, they wanted to build a community, with low rise townhouse style units, connected by walkways and alleys. The designed a U-shaped road, that we called "the horse shoe" which went through the main part of the project, but there were some houses which were only accessible through a walkway. The result was lots of sneaky paths, alleys and hiding spots that made it easy for drug dealers to move throughout the housing project and elude police.

Because Sursum Corda was so active with the drug trade, it was especially important to us that we had the Club, a true space for kids. But, like everything else in my neighborhood, there was always a little bit of bad hiding in there with the good.

The Club was led by a tall and imposing black man named Jimmy Watkins. He was a retired policeman, with a kind wife and a special interest in helping the kids at the Club to see a future for themselves. He was my first basketball coach, and the one who coached me the longest, since I continued to play Club basketball through high school.

My first basketball team was the U8 team, which was for six and seven-year-old boys. I followed Earl to practice when I was just five. I sat on the sidelines when Coach Jimmy ran the practice, and I would jump on the court with my ball when there was a break. Sometimes Jimmy let me practice with them, and other times he had me sit out.

I remember when the boys got white uniform t-shirts that had Metropolitan Police Boys & Girls Club #2 on the front and I wanted one in the worst way. The team had an away game at Georgetown University one day, and I followed Earl hoping I could go. I was surprised and elated when Jimmy threw me a white shirt and said, "Ok Eric, you're going!" and ushered me into the van with the other boys for the trip across town.

Our Club played during half time at the early season exhibition games for the Georgetown Hoyas. The Hoyas played at the Cap Center at that time, but the first few games of the season were played on campus in McDonough Arena, and our Club scrimmage was the halftime show. Legendary Hoya coach John Thompson was a DC guy who had been involved with our Club as a child. He invited us to the games and let us meet the players in the locker room.

During those years when I was six, seven and eight years old, I met basketball superstars such as Dikembe Mutombo, Alonzo Mourning and Allen Iverson, all at Georgetown games with my Club teammates.

Coach Jimmy had us under tight control, there was no misbehaving. I remember one time, after our half time exhibition, we sat on the bench in our white uniform t-shirts, looking straight ahead as Coach talked to us. "You have to stay with your man," he said, "And move that ball around, don't shoot until you have an opening!"

But just then John Thompson walked out of the locker room, leading the players right past us. They were walking behind our bench, just inches from us. Coach Jimmy gave us look, which seemed to tell us we better stay seated and focused. But one boy on the team stuck his hand up for a high five without turning his head. He was focused on Coach Jimmy and looking right at him, but he also had his hand out behind him, hoping for a high five. We all copied him, with

12 little hands nervously sticking out behind us looking for acknowledgement from the big guys. Alonzo Mourning and the other players walked by and high fived us, without losing their focus as they got ready to start their second half. The Hoyas were THE team in Washington DC for kids from my neighborhood. We loved everything about them and that was the high five of a life time.

Coach Jimmy loved the Hoyas too and we were all a little surprised that we didn't get a beating for asking for a high five when we were supposed to be looking straight ahead. You see, Coach Jimmy was a good influence in my life, but also a complicated one. He was not shy about beating the kids at Club #2.

Jimmy had a wooden paddle and he would lay a kid across his lap and smack you four times with it. He paddled kids who fought or talked back or used curse words. He paddled me for all of those offenses, and one time for riding my bike onto the basketball court. I got a new bike for Christmas when I was seven, and I wanted to ride it around the gym and show it off. It made everyone laugh and I enjoyed it, but I got the paddle for it.

He used to beat kids who wore Polo Ralph Lauren clothes. He thought that Ralph Lauren was racist, and he didn't like to see black children wearing Polo, so if you showed up to the Club with it, you got paddled. Even the toughest gangstas at Sursum Corda had a level of respect for Jimmy since certain things were just not tolerated at the club, and he was a commanding male presence in our neighborhood.

Not only did I get paddled at the Club, I also got kicked out for days or weeks at a time. I liked mischief and messing around with people, so I was frequently disciplined. But the thing is, Jimmy loved me for basketball. I was phenomenal when I was that age, and I turned a lot of heads at games. I was barred from the Club, but as soon as it was basketball time, Jimmy would tolerate my behavior and let me back in no matter what I did. I never got banned from the Club during basketball season.

Jimmy was my first coach and I learned the fundamentals of basketball from him. I learned discipline and how to focus on the game. I played for Club #2 for eight years, and I never lost a game during all that time. When I was eight or nine years old, AAU coaches started to notice me and there was talk about me.

From then on, Coach Jimmy would remind me every time I saw him, "I'm your agent! Don't forget!"

He said it warmly, and there were many years when I was so little and naïve to these topics, that I thought that he actually was my agent and was making some plans on my behalf.

When basketball started to bring me positive attention, I began to see the trouble around me only as noise. I tried to avoid it. When I played at Georgetown at the half time in front of the big crowd, I would feel moments of pride, thinking that good things awaited me.

Chapter Two

My world opened up a little wider one fall afternoon when I was nine years old. Rob Jackson, a coach with a top AAU travel program, came to scout me at Club #2. I knew he was watching me, so I picked up my game and showed as much intensity as I could. Coach Rob was with the Blue Devils, an AAU basketball program that sponsored teams for various age groups, from 10U to 18U. My brother Earl was already on a Blue Devils team, but with a different coach, so I was familiar with what it involved, and I was extremely interested.

Rob was a sharp, well put-together black man, who was intelligent, confident, and had come to Sursum Corda to speak directly to me. It was the first time I had encountered a man like that, and I was so taken with how he presented himself and what he was saying to me. I was used to the neighborhood guys, and Rob was different. He talked about the Blue Devils basketball program and he said things that people had never told me before.

"You are good, Eric,", he said, "but you can be better."

"Ok," I said, and nodded.

I was used to adults telling me that I was extremely good at basketball. They warned me to behave myself so that I could have a future in the sport—a college scholarship and a career in the NBA. I saw the look of wonder or amazement when they watched me play, and I heard them talk to each other about how I could be famous someday. But I had never heard anyone say that I had things to work on. At that age, I didn't understand basketball success to be something one worked toward; I thought it was all about talent. Either you had it, or you didn't.

"You need to work on your jump shot," Rob said, "and I can help you with that. Our team travels, and we play the best competition that we can find. That's another thing that will help you to get better."

The idea that there was better competition out there was exciting to me. My understanding of what travel teams were all about was limited at age nine, but when I heard about tournaments, gym time, travel teams, uniforms; those were all words and ideas that interested me. I was in.

I joined the Blue Devils and practiced with Rob and his team at Boys & Girls Clubs and at the Tacoma Park Recreation Center in Maryland. I learned a lot about basketball, but I also learned how to present myself and how to behave. Rob became a life-long role model and mentor to me.

On car rides to practice and tournaments, we talked about our daily lives and things going on in the world.

Rob had a consulting job of some kind, and coached basketball on the side. He had a wife and daughter at home. He didn't have a big background in basketball, but he was one of the best coaches I have ever had because of his focus on motivation, team work and life skills. In my eyes, Rob did everything at a higher level than I was used to seeing. He was on time, engaged and involved and always giving his best to us. He required us to work hard, be honest, and treat others well. I watched how Rob interacted with people and I learned a lot from him.

At this time, I continued to play Club #2 basketball for Coach Jimmy and I also played on the CYO team at my school, Holy Redeemer. My elementary school years were spent at this small Catholic school located just next to Sursum Corda. It was a typical parish school with lots of structure and order. The student body was predominately black, and most of them came from low income families who paid with vouchers, scholarships, or monthly payment plans.

My mother felt strongly about sending me and Earl to Catholic school, even though we were not members of that church. She had attended Catholic school herself and was always a good student. But she transferred to our local public high school, Dunbar, in eleventh grade, and thought that it had complicated things in her life. She wanted us to have the best education possible, one with serious students and the best teachers. Our local public option was

Walker Jones Elementary, which had a reputation of being fun and crazy, but not much work was done there. Instead, Earl and I enrolled at Holy Redeemer. Our mother paid our tuition each month, which came from her salary as a postal employee. Earl and I wore our clip-on ties, navy blue pants and light blue dress shirts every day; and I felt important and ready for school in my uniform.

I always had an urge to surround myself with smart or successful people. Even though I did goof off at Holy Redeemer, I also tried to be the best student in my class. I sat with the smart girls when I could, and I envied their neat handwriting. I wanted to be the best at everything. I was a very competitive person.

But our class was far behind. In fifth grade, there were some students who were still learning to read. There were children who could not focus or pay attention, and the environment was one in which our class could only focus on learning for short periods of time.

When I got bored, I would act up, or join in the fun or messing around that was going on in class. My fifth-grade teacher was Mr. Sweata, a very serious man, and I remember putting chalk in his coffee when he wasn't looking and laughing so hard when he drank it. I also put a tack on his chair and he screamed when he sat on it.

I wanted more for myself than Holy Redeemer School could offer. There was one better option that I knew about, and that was Holy Trinity School in

Georgetown. A group of five Sursum Corda students traveled across the city each day to attend this elementary school which was just a block away from the Georgetown University campus. My cousin Kim was one of the lucky few who attended this school which was known for its rigorous curriculum and friendly, welcoming environment. The Holy Trinity students were mostly white, from upper middle-class families, and many of them commuted from the suburbs. I remember being most impressed with the fact that the Holy Trinity students used the Yates Field House on the Georgetown campus for their gym classes.

The path to the Holy Trinity scholarship opportunity started with the Georgetown tutors. Sursum Corda and Georgetown University had a partnership that lasted over forty years. The Sursum Corda housing development was built and sponsored by Catholics, including the Jesuits at the neighboring Gonzaga High School. The Jesuits are an order of the Catholic church known for education and social justice, so it was not surprising that as soon as Sursum Corda was built, they were sending tutors from both Gonzaga High School and Georgetown University to work with the children. The Catholics named the housing development Sursum Corda, which means "lift up your hearts" in Latin and is a response in the Catholic mass.

Even my mother had a Georgetown tutor. In those days, the tutors came together on a van and then went to their student's house and tutored right at the kitchen table. By the 1990s, when I got my first Georgetown tutor, all the kids and tutors met together in the community center in a second-floor room above the laundry room. I remember seeing the Georgetown van pull into the horseshoe and running over with the other kids. We would look into the van windows and wave, hoping to see our tutor. The van came to Sursum Corda four nights a week, but each child met his or her tutor only once a week.

I scanned the windows and yelled "yes!" and pumped my fist when I saw my tutor Kristin.

I started working with Kristin as my tutor when I was a four-year-old kindergartener. I loved to sit beside her, eat the apple or snack that she brought me, and read with her. There was a lot of noise going on around us, since the room was full of about twenty other kid and tutor pairs. Some kid would break free and run to the piano to bang on it, so there was always happy noise and chaos during tutoring, but we managed to get a lot done.

The tutors published a literary magazine for us each year, which included our best poem or writing from the year. The children loved to see their names in print, and we admired the colorful cover and this very important looking publication that we got to take home with us. When I was seven, I contributed this poem to the Sursum Corda Literary Magazine.

Playing Ball
By Eric Price, age 7
I like basketball, the court is very tall.
If I dunk it, I will fall.
The best season is fall, I like to play ball.
Don't forget the court is very tall,
And last week, I went to the mall,
So that I could buy a new basketball.

Kristin was my tutor when I was in kindergarten through third grade. She read with me during tutoring sessions, but also took me out on the weekends for little trips with other tutors and kids. We visited the Georgetown campus, saw the Washington DC Christmas tree lighting, went bowling and enjoyed the annual picnic for all the kids in the program. At the end of my third-grade year, my mother took me to Kristin's graduation from Georgetown. When she was called to the stage to get her diploma, I cheered as loud as I could. More than twenty years later, Kristin and I are still in touch, and she is helping me write my story. She is an example of one of the many mentors in my life that helped me to keep moving forward in a positive way.

Georgetown tutors were important to the entire Sursum Corda community. I was not the only one who benefitted from this relationship, there are so many stories of lasting connections and positive memories of tutoring. The tutors brought a sense of hope to the community. It was uplifting because someone who was already in college, was showing interest in us. They came all the way across town to meet specifically with one small child. They encouraged us, and they showed us that reading was important. Their time and attention let us know that we were important, that we mattered to people outside our community. The tutors were a cross section of Georgetown students, and they came from all over the country and the world. We asked them a lot of questions, and their presence and attention helped us to see beyond Sursum Corda and the world we knew.

Holy Trinity School is located a block from the main gates of Georgetown University, in a neighborhood with brightly colored townhouses and student apartments. My tutor, Kristin, thought I was a good candidate for Holy Trinity. One day she walked me back to my house to talk to my mother.

"I think Eric should apply to Holy Trinity" she said, handing my mom a folder with a brochure, course catalog and general information on the school. "He is a strong reader and a good student and could use a greater challenge."

"My neice goes there," my mom answered, "I would love for Eric to go too. What can we do from here?"

Kristin told my mom about the application process, and I grabbed the folder with the information on Holy Trinity School. I read it from front to back, over and over again, wanting to know everything I could about it. Even at nine years old, I perceived that this school was "better", and there was a sense of excellence that I wanted to be a part of. I became determined to get accepted to Holy Trinity.

I visited the school in fourth grade for my interview and admissions test. Kristin helped me and my mother with the process of completing forms and coordinating with Holy Redeemer for teacher recommendations. I was selected to apply for admission based on my grades, reading level, and performance in the Georgetown tutoring program. It didn't have anything to do with basketball, although there were students or parents who thought that I was getting a basketball scholarship. There was a lot of talk, but I tried to put it out of my mind.

In the spring, I was notified that there was not enough room for me in the fifth-grade class. I was so disappointed, and I didn't fully understand the reasoning.

Kristin tried to explain by saying, "There are not enough desks in the fifth grade, so you can't go this year."

I answered, "I can get a desk from Holy Redeemer and bring it over. We have so many extra desks!"

It was a setback to be denied admission for the fifth grade. I had wanted to attend so badly, that it was hard to believe that it wasn't going to happen. However, Kristin told me that the sixth grade at Holy

Trinity added another section and they accepted an additional twenty students, so I would have a good chance the next year. I promised myself that I would keep my grades up, do my best at basketball and stay out of trouble so that I could get into Holy Trinity in sixth grade.

Chapter Three

By the spring of 1997, my 10U Blue Devils team was rolling through all our tournaments without giving up a game. We played the PG Jaguars, Run N Slam and other teams on the AAU circuit in DC and beat them all. We drove to Virginia and North Carolina for weekend tournaments and maintained our undefeated status. Rob was proud of our team work and how we had all improved throughout the year.

"I have good news for y'all" he told us one day at practice, "We qualified for Nationals! We are going to Disney!"

A trip to Disney World for a major basketball tournament was a dream come true for all of us. We were jumping and dancing with excitement. It was the first year that the AAU National Championships would be held at the new Disney Wide World of Sports Arena in Orlando. Plans were made, money was raised, and soon we were caravanning down to Orlando by car.

We stayed in a hotel; three boys to a room, and that in itself was a thrill. With 54 teams in the tournament, the hotel and basketball venue were swarming with nine and ten-year-old boys. The vibe was one of excitement, friendship, fun, and competitiveness. The Blue

Devils had earned the number one seed in the tournament, and we were known to be the team to beat.

The event started with the lighting of a torch and an opening ceremony presided over by the president of AAU. He said, "Of the 556 players competing in this week's 10 and Under basketball tournament, the odds are that only three of you will become professional basketball players."

My teammates and I nudged each other and laughed. "He hasn't seen us yet!" one guy whispered. We fully believed that we would all be in the NBA one day.

Other teams knew that we were the number one seeded team and gathered around our court to watch us warm up. One boy asked for my autograph, and his coach got mad at him for doing that. Another team stared at us as we walked onto the court to play them, making their coach say, "Stop looking at them that way! They are going to know you are scared!"

We won our early round games easily. We made it to the final four with the Charlotte Stars, which was a team we hung out with a lot. We had water gun fights with them in the hotel hallways. Steph Curry was the nine-year-old point guard of the Charlotte Stars. I remember him because his father was NBA player Dell Curry. It made me play tougher, to guard his son harder, when I knew that this pro basketball star was watching me.

The Blue Devils team played hard, and we played smart. Rob was not an animated, screaming from the sidelines type of coach, but he was an integral part of our wins. In the semifinals, we played a team from Richmond, and they had an early lead on us. Three of our starters fouled out of the game. I was still in it at the end, and we pressed hard, and ended up coming from behind to win 52-49.

In the finals, we found ourselves facing the Charlotte Stars. We were down by 16 points in the third quarter, but again, we were able to rally. Our up-tempo game and strong defense helped us to take the lead and we won, 55-53. It was an intense game and a thrilling victory. We really came together as a team, we did everything we had practiced, and we refused to give up when we were down.

We were the 10U AAU National Champions, and after the game we went to, you guessed it, Disney World. I was named tournament MVP. It meant so much to me to be recognized that way, and as a competitive person, I always wanted to be the best out there, so it felt good when others recognized it. The online recruiting services and bloggers gave me my first national ranking. They said I was the number one 10-year-old basketball player in the country. I don't know what business people have ranking ten-year-olds, but it felt amazing at the time. I was so proud. I left the tournament feeling like anything was possible in life.

The summer of 1997, when I was 10 years old, turned out to be a real turning point in my life. Not only did

I have great success in basketball, but I started summer school at Holy Trinity. I had been accepted for the sixth grade, with a requirement that I attend a summer program. The five of us from Sursum Corda took two public buses across town each day, to attend classes in reading and math taught by Miss McNulty. She was a kind young teacher who became our champion at the school. She worked as hard as we did with a goal of helping us to succeed at Holy Trinity.

There was another new sixth grader from Sursum Corda, and he was my close friend Morris Mitchell. I was more confident knowing that I was going into a new school with a friend I could rely on. Morris and I loved the summer school program. It was a special feeling to step off that bus in Georgetown, with the cobblestone streets, the brightly colored town houses. It was a neighborhood with a sense of history and achievement, and I was proud to be part of it.

Traveling to Georgetown each day for my sixth-grade year took me out of Sursum Corda in a meaningful way. With all the time I spent traveling to school during the week, and going to basketball practices on weekends, I didn't have as much time to hang out with the kids in the neighborhood. I stopped the antics and petty crime of my earlier childhood. I had moved forward athletically and academically, and I was feeling confident in myself.

My first day of school at Holy Trinity was all that I had hoped it would be. I put on my uniform, which was khaki pants and a navy-blue polo shirt, a more preppy version of the Catholic school uniform I was used to. I met Morris and his sister Helen, and then the others and we headed to the bus stop. We arrived in Georgetown and walked up O Street and could hear the children playing in the street which was blocked off for morning recess. Morris and I joined in and felt welcomed.

I noticed that the classroom behavior was different from what I was used to. The kids listened to the teacher and responded frequently with questions and comments that were on topic. There was talking at times, but nothing egregious and it was a lot calmer and quieter than I had expected. There were zero behavior issues at Holy Trinity and I had to adapt to that. I could not goof off or act out, or I would be an outcast. No one acted that way and there was no room for me to do that. I changed my classroom behavior immediately and acted as the others did.

I was excited to go to Holy Trinity. People looked at me a little differently, but I didn't really notice, or care, at first, since I wanted to be there so badly. It was like momentum in my life. I wanted to show people and myself that it wasn't just basketball, but also academics that I was good at. I wanted to prove to myself that I could work on this level and I wanted to be around smart kids.

Having Morris with me really helped. I knew I had a friend there. There were two of us, and I always had someone to sit with or support me. Miss McNulty called us "Frick and Frack" since we were always together. I felt like I was a part of a team. I had Miss McNulty who was on my side and helped me navigate the school both socially and academically. I had the four other Sursum Corda kids who would stick by me and show me the way when I needed it. It turned out that the entire school community was supportive of our group from Sursum Corda. Teachers were friendly and helpful, parents included us in parties and events and drove us around, and the students treated us like any other kids.

I remember the feeling I had on that first day when I walked into my homeroom and noticed a small Washington Post article hanging on the bulletin board. My Blue Devils team had made it into the paper after our National Championships; and it included a team picture and an article about our fantastic run in the spring and our win at the big tournament in Orlando. I couldn't believe that my homeroom teacher had noticed it, and that she decided to hang it in the classroom for everyone to see. It was so kind and welcoming, that I knew this school was everything I had hoped it would be.

I had a teacher named Mr. Hennessey who was passionate about history and used different ways to help us to understand what he was teaching. There was a boy named Christian in my class who was a super smart kid. He always seemed to know what he was talking about and had special insights that the others didn't have. On one of the first days, Mr., Hennessey assigned a chapter to read for homework. I just breezed through it and looked it over. The next day, it was evident that Christian had read. He asked questions, he pulled out facts from the text to make his point. I had never seen anyone do this. I thought, man, this guy is not coming to play. All the kids at Holy Trinity were smart, but Christian was above and beyond. He was clearly ahead of me, and it inspired me to try to keep up. I realized that he knew a lot of things because he read, and he prepared for class. It made me think that I needed to read, and I needed to spend more time on the homework. Christian challenged me and struck a competitive chord in me, making me try to do better.

Most of my classmates were from high income families, including several black students who were children of lawyers and business professionals. Some of them lived in the suburbs, and their mothers were kind enough to drive me home after a sleep-over or party. I made friends easily and Morris and I were often invited to playdates and parties in Virginia and Maryland.

One time, I was in the car with a white friend and his little brother. The boy, who was three or four years old, was strapped into his car seat. He looked at me and said, "Eric, are you black?"

"Yes," I said.

"Ewww!" he replied, making a face.

His mother and brother jumped in immediately with harsh words, embarrassment, and apologies to me. I felt bad, but I understood he was very young. It felt awkward that my friend and his mother were so embarrassed and were scolding the boy and apologizing to me.

But other than that incident, I felt comfortable at Holy Trinity, and very much embraced by the students, parents, and faculty. I was able to find several mentors at this stage in my life. Miss McNulty was my math teacher, but also the one in charge of the Sursum Corda after school homework help program. She was with us every day and she really believed in us. I often wondered who would work that hard to bring the best out of someone? She did everything for us, she encouraged and helped us, and pushed us. I still can't believe that someone did that for me. We put a lot of stress on her, but she thought about us all the time and believed in us. If I ever started to doubt myself, there she was believing in me, and working so hard with us, I knew I could do more.

Mr. Hennessey is another mentor who taught me how to do higher level school work. He had high standards for me yet put no pressure on me. He would say, "It may look like a lot of work, but you can do it, Eric." I never felt alone there, I had so much support and encouragement.

Winter basketball season started, and I continued to play for Coach Jimmy at the Boys & Girls Club. He was encouraging and positive with me and he continued his signature line with me, which was "Don't forget, I'm your agent!" My team won all its games that season, just as we had in all the previous years.

I went to tryouts for the sixth-grade basketball team at Holy Trinity. The coach quickly moved me up to the eighth-grade team and I loved the chance to play with the oldest boys in the school. I didn't turn 11 years old until basketball season was fully under way in late December, so I was a skinny pre-teen playing with the 13 and 14-year-olds. and still dominating on the court.

My old coach from Holy Redeemer School saw me around the neighborhood and was disappointed that I had changed schools. He tried to convince me to continue to play for him at Holy Redeemer. Earl was playing for him on the seventh-grade team, and he tried to coax me back by saying I could join my brother and we would have the best team in the league. He was relentless with his request, asking Earl and the other players to try their best to get me back.

I went up to Miss McNulty after school and sheepishly asked her, "Can I play on the Holy Redeemer basketball team but still go to school here?" It was a half-hearted request, since I loved my new school so much.

She talked with me, trying to get to the bottom of why I was asking this. I am not sure if I even knew why I asked her. My old coach had been so convincing and so commanding in his request for me to play for him at Holy Redeemer. It was the first of many times that a coach put his own interests and his own demands ahead of what was best for me.

I played for Holy Trinity, and I loved hearing the cheering crowds, and being part of the team. So many of the students and parents came to watch the games, that it brought an exciting vibe to the gym. I played point guard and I passed a lot, getting everyone involved, and trying my best to make all the other guys look good. I felt like I was bringing something to the community, that I was being embraced for who I was, and I so proud to be a part of it.

Chapter Four

On the first day of spring practice with Blue Devils, I saw this giant 11-year-old boy, who was about 6'3, walk into the gym. We were high fiving and gave a little cheer to see such a big man joining our team. His name was Roy Hibbert and by the time he was 12, he was 6'6. He finally topped out at 7'2 and played college ball at Georgetown. He went on to have a nine-year career in the NBA playing for the Indiana Pacers, Denver Nuggets, and several other teams. Roy was a solid player at age eleven but didn't have the athleticism or speed that the other guys had. He was growing into his body and still had a lot to learn.

Ty Lawson was a new guard on the Blue Devils. He and I got along well and we both liked the up-tempo style of play that Rob showed us. Ty went on to play for the North Carolina Tarheels, then to the NBA with the Denver Nuggets. He is back in DC playing with the Washington Wizards now.

We also had Dante Cunningham, who was on the 10U team with me as well. Dante was always a fast and smart player. He went to Villanova, then on to the Portland Trailblazers and several other NBA teams.

It's not surprising that the Blue Devils won so often, considering I had three future NBA players on the court with me. We played a heavy spring schedule of games all over the east coast. We were shocked with one loss, and that hit us hard. But we put it behind us and moved forward with our season. We qualified for the 1999 AAU National Championships in Orlando and made plans to travel there in August.

Our team was sponsored by Nike, which meant that we received free gear and shoes. I believe that Rob got a salary or stipend of some kind, but our travel was not fully paid for by Nike. With older players, Nike had what we called "circuit teams," that played the entire Nike summer circuit with travel expenses covered. Our Blue Devils 11U team covered some of its travel through fundraising and player donations. I know that my mother didn't pay anything for me.

The AAU National Championships was full of excited energy and familiar faces. We cruised through the first few games. In the semi-final, we played a team from Texas that was strong, with a guard named Byron Eaton who went on to play for Oklahoma State. We ran a full court press, and it worked so well because we had speed, intensity, and a big man in back court. When our opponent took the ball out, we pressed. Ty and Dante put on the pressure, and I was the fast guy waiting in the middle of the zone. The pressure caused them to pass too quickly, and I would be waiting right in the middle of the zone to steal it. Their guy didn't know where he was throwing the ball, he was under so much pressure. The key to running this successfully is that you need a big man all the way in the back and a fast man in the middle of the zone, and the other three guys up front creating havoc. We did it brilliantly, and no one could get past us.

In that semi-final game, I had the unique distinction of scoring a quadruple double. It's unusual for a basketball player at any level to get a quadruple double, so it was thrilling to me when I heard I had achieved it. The more common designation is a triple double, where you reach double digits in three out of the five game stats—points, assists, steals, rebounds, or blocked shots. On that big day, I got a quadruple double, scoring thirty points, with twelve assists, eleven steals, and ten rebounds.

My strength in basketball was that I had what some coaches called "good court sense". I had a knack of visualizing plays and knowing everyone else's position, and even sensing where they would go before they moved. I had a level of concentration and ability to see the whole court that most other kids didn't have at age eleven. I also had a strong inner voice and will to win. When I was on the basketball court, I always knew that each individual player needs to win his own individual battle. I focused on dominating the player in front of me. At that age, I had the belief that not one player on this earth could stop me from getting to the basket. I didn't care if it was Michael Jordan himself, I never believed that one player could come between me and the basketball hoop.

Rob taught me game management, tempo and speed. In practice, I played all positions so that I would know and get a feel of where people were on the court. We ran a pro-style offense, so plays were not really scripted, which gave me the ability to use my judgement and react to what was happening on the court.

One other advantage that I had was height. I was 5'7 when I was eleven years old. I wasn't as big as some of the forwards like Roy Hibbert, but I was usually the biggest guard out there. Dante and Ty were strong players, but when we were eleven, I was more than half a foot taller than they were, and being bigger, stronger, and faster helped me to dominate. Ty was so small that it was hard for him to create his own shot. I remember having a little bit of a bad feeling one day in middle school when I heard the adults marveling over Dante's shoe size. I was six feet tall when I was twelve, but I wore a size nine shoe. I was taller than Dante, but he wore size 16 shoes. It was obvious he had a long way to go in terms of growth, but for me, we weren't so sure.

I loved the independence that my travels brought me. My mom never came to the away games since she was a single parent of three and had a full-time job. Roy, Dante, and Ty, they always had their parents with them. They had guidance. They were practicing when we didn't have practice. They had a father figure who was with them all the time. It didn't bother me that my mom couldn't come, I was on top of the world, and I liked being on my own. Rob was a father figure to me, he was like my dad. When we drove to tournaments or practices, I would sit in the front seat with Rob, everyone knew that I had shotgun. At dinner on the road, the other boys might sit with their parents, but I would sit with Rob. He meant a lot to me and was a positive influence at a critical time in my life.

There was always some trouble going on at Sursum Corda. Some of my friends from home, age 11 or 12, started selling drugs and getting caught up in the system. Some were using and abusing drugs. There were kids my age who missed school a lot, staying out at night, getting too far away from a healthy routine and lifestyle. It was difficult to see old friends slipping away from me. Yet I held tightly onto the fact that I had something. I had basketball, which was already taking me out of Sursum Corda both physically and emotionally, making it easier to distance myself from trouble.

This was about the time of my life when I became famous at Sursum Corda. Everyone wanted to be my friend. Adults saw dollar signs, even before I did, and wanted to find a way to get close to me. There were adults who talked with me about working as my agent or manager.

Some adults couldn't even clarify what they wanted

from me. "Don't forget me when you're famous, Toe!",
they would say, using my neighborhood nickname
which I got for being pigeon-toed.

My mother woke me up one morning with exciting
news. "Toe!" she called up to me, "You are going to be
in Sports Illustrated! Wake up! I have the best news!"

I jumped out of bed and ran down the stairs, "What
are you talking about? How do you know?"

"Some lady from Sports Illustrated for Kids just
called and they are going to do a full-page photo spread
on you! You are going to be in Sports Illustrated!" My
mom screamed. She and my sister Shanika were jumping up and down and doing a little dance.

It turned out that the magazine wanted to do a
story on me because of my quadruple double in the
AAU National Championships. They were sending a
photo crew and reporter to the Boys & Girls Club in
my neighborhood.

If you can imagine what it felt like to be an eleven-
year-old boy walking into your Sports Illustrated photo
shoot, it was almost too much to handle. The Club was
closed to everyone else while the photographers set up
in the gym. Parents, kids, and even the gangstas in the
neighborhood made their way to the Club to see what
they could get a glimpse of.

"Toe, are you filming a commercial?" one kid asked me.

"Any famous people coming to this, Toe? Dick
Vitale interviewing you?" another kid asked.

"Good luck Eric, and God bless you," one of the moms said to me.

I could feel the sense of pride from my neighbors. These were people who had to endure shootings, violence, and difficult circumstances on a daily basis. Yet they saw photographers and a journalist coming to their neighborhood to talk with one of their own, a boy who was doing something good with his life and was getting national level recognition. They wanted to be a part of it, in some small way. So, they gathered in front of the Boys & Girls Club and watched from the sidewalk.

My mom and I went into the gym and talked to the team from Sports Illustrated. They had asked me to wear my Blue Devils uniform jersey, so I did. They asked me about my experience at the tournament, my teammates, and to what I attributed such success on the court. They took a lot of pictures of me dribbling and shooting.

Finally, one photographer had the idea of getting a ladder and climbing above the rim. He asked me to do a layup, and to look up above the basket and smile. I did it twice, and he seemed satisfied and said, "That's the winner."

It was several months before the article was published. I was surprised that no one from Sports Illustrated for Kids mailed me a copy or called me to let me know it was out. I checked at the news stand at Union Station continually for months. Finally, one day, there it was.

It was a full-page picture of me, doing the layup. The article said that I was 11 years old, 5'7, and a guard for the Potomac Blue Devils AAU team.

It included a comment about me being a "defensive whiz" on the basketball court, then concluded with a quote from me saying, "Scoring points is fun, but playing good defense is how you win games."

"Hey, Eric and Earl!" a coach called out to us, "Can I talk to you for a minute?"

This was usually how the conversation started. A coach would come to our game or approach us after a practice at the Club. High school coaches from the Washington Catholic Athletic Conference, such as DeMatha, St. John's or Archbishop Carroll would meet us after Holy Trinity or Holy Redeemer games. Coaches for the small start-up Christian schools, such as National Christian, Riverdale Baptist, or Montrose Christian, would find us at the Club. We also heard from coaches from rival AAU travel teams, and one time a boarding school coach came to talk to us. We were sometimes approached by people who claimed to be agents or have some insight or idea for us, but we really weren't sure who they were and what they wanted.

"I'm a coach at National Christian School," he said, "We would love to have you guys come and play for us."

Earl asked him, "Who is on your team? What teams do you play?"

The coach told us about his players and the program. Then he added, "I know you two are looked at as a package deal. Where one brother goes to high school, the other one will go too. But hey, you are both point guards. It might make sense for y'all to split up. Think about it, and please think about National Christian," he said.

He was right, it was assumed that Earl and I were going to the same high school. My brother started to get recruited in seventh grade, so I went along on some of the visits. I had never given any thought to the fact that we both played the same position and could end up being rivals. And even after this coach mentioned it to us, it didn't really sink in. I felt invincible. Nothing would stop me from playing at the top. I assumed I would overtake Earl at some point, but I didn't see it as a problem, I saw it as a victory. I liked the idea of my brother and I on the same team.

I also never considered how Earl felt about my success in basketball. Earl was very good in his own right, with a national ranking and great skills on the court. But my star had taken off in the last two years and I don't know how he felt about that. As a kid, I saw him as my cool older brother, and I didn't realize until later that this could be a source of conflict.

It was at the height of my success and attention that Earl decided to quit the Blue Devils and join a rival team. Whether it was the allure of something better, the persuasiveness of the coach, or just simply that he wanted to do something different from me, his little brother, I don't know. But he came home one day and told me and my mother that he was joining a team called DC Assault.

The world of travel teams, summer league, AAU ball, or whatever you wanted to call it, was like the wild west, anything goes. Some of the coaches had dollar signs in their eyes and promoted their teams with the idea of getting players to the NBA and cashing out somehow. In the short term, if they had good results they could get sponsored by Adidas or Nike and a coaching salary from a sneaker company.

Under Armor was not yet on the scene, so the rivalry was strictly Nike versus Adidas. The big-name players in the 18U age group made national headlines, and they were either on a Nike team, playing the Nike summer tour, in tournaments like the Nike Big Time in Las Vegas or the Peach Jam in South Carolina, while Adidas guys played at the famous Adidas ABCD camp in New Jersey. These tournaments were the ticket to college scholarships and connections with NBA scouts.

Earl met a guy named Curtis Malone who ran the DC Assault basketball program. Curtis was 27 years old, a street guy, with an ability to read people and to connect with them. What most people knew about Curtis in 1998 was that he had one of the best AAU teams in the country. He had DerMarr Johnson and Keith Bogans, the two top recruits in the country, along with James White, another future NBA player.

One basketball analyst called the team a "high wire act" since they were wowing crowds with their above the rim play.

But what people didn't know about Curtis then was that he had a drug conviction and he didn't have much basketball experience. But I'm not sure anyone would have even cared, since his ability to attract and motivate talent was unprecedented. Curtis Malone had played basketball in high school, then went to college for a semester, but dropped out. He started selling drugs and was arrested for distribution of crack cocaine. When he got out of prison, he became interested in coaching grass roots basketball and teamed up with a friend named Troy Weaver. They assembled a team of elite talent very quickly and found their stars rising. Weaver left for other positions in basketball, but Curtis stayed with DC Assault.

It wasn't hard to convince Earl to join Curtis and the DC Assault 14U team. Curtis put DerMarr Johnson on the phone with my brother one time and it was done. DerMarr Johnson was a legend in our circle. He was a McDonald's All-American, Parade High School Player of the Year, and a DC guy, just like us. He talked to Earl and told him what a great program DC Assault was, and Earl was sold.

Chapter Five

Our Blue Devils team was as strong as ever, but we did not win a third consecutive national title. We went to Orlando, played well in the tournament, but we lost in the finals to a strong team from Dallas. I was so pissed off about it after the loss, that I couldn't stop thinking about it.

We rode the van back to the hotel in awkward silence. Finally, Roy Hibbert blurted out, "I'm hungry! Can we eat?"

I got angry and lashed out at Roy, "How can you think about eating! We just lost!"

Roy knew that basketball was just a game and you win some and you lose some. And as a 12-year-old who was 6'6, he probably really did need to eat. I always took losing very personally, and it affected me deeply, more than it should have.

At the end of the summer, I returned to Holy Trinity for eighth grade. I was finally at the top, the oldest grade in the school, and it was my third year, so I had adjusted to the academic rigor, and I found a place for myself in the community.

Raymond, my mom's boyfriend, came into my life

at this time. At first it was hard to accept him because my mom would try to push it on me saying that he was a great guy and good for all of us. But in time, Raymond became a father figure to me. My mom was right about Raymond, even though it took me a while to realize it. He was a bus driver for the city, very responsible, and he treated all four of us so well. Raymond was the example of how to be a good husband that I looked to when I got married myself.

Gonzaga College High School was right next to Sursum Corda, so I grew up seeing boys in purple jackets walking from Union Station down to the school every day. Some of the boys came to Sursum Corda to tutor us, and we neighborhood kids were invited to the school to watch sports or other events.

I was on track to get admitted to Gonzaga and get a scholarship there even without basketball. Since I had been selected by the Georgetown tutors for a Holy Trinity scholarship, and I had done well academically, the next step was to go to a Jesuit high school, or any school that I was admitted to. I had an existing relationship at Gonzaga, so I always had it in my mind that I would probably go there.

Earl and I were welcomed by the basketball and admissions team and spent many afternoons at the school going to "open gym" and getting homework help. In the spring, when basketball had ended, the Gonzaga basketball team had open gym workouts and they also had a loosely organized study hall. Earl and I were encouraged to take part in this, even though we were only in middle school. I loved the chance to play against the big guys, and I went as often as I could.

I got to know Bill Whitaker, who was the director of admissions and an assistant basketball coach. He was a young coach who was good at bringing out the best in everyone. I could tell that his interest in me and Earl was not only for basketball. He knew we had so many voices in our ears and he was able to get to our level and really talk with us, and to listen to what we had to say. Many of our conversations ended with him saying, "Remember, you need a plan for what to do when that basketball stops bouncing."

The decision of which high school to attend brought up the issue of my early birthday. I would be only 13 when I started ninth grade, turning 14 at the end of December. Boys in wealthier communities would have attended Pre-Kindergarten, and then started kindergarten at age 5, and high school at 14 or even 15, something they call "red shirting." I didn't have that option in Sursum Corda. We didn't have a Pre-K program, and families near us couldn't have afforded it anyway. Children with birthdays that were late in the calendar year went to kindergarten at age four, since it was better to get them in school rather than have them sitting at home. But at the private schools I attended, red-shirting for kindergarten was the norm, and thus I was significantly younger than the other students.

From a college sports point of view, there is a benefit to being older. Starting college at age 17 in a Division I sports program is not common. I was told by coaches that I should consider repeating eighth grade or finding some way to "re-classify." It was ultimately a decision that I put off. I was excited for the challenge of high school basketball and there was no way I wanted to stay in eighth grade for another year.

Gonzaga was my likely choice, but there was one other school that was a big contender for me. DeMatha Catholic High School was a basketball powerhouse at that time. Coach Morgan Wooten was the one of the only high school coaches to be inducted into the Basketball Hall of Fame and was nationally known by everyone in the basketball world.

A visit was arranged for me, and I went to DeMatha during my eighth-grade year. I sat down with Coach Wooten and his son and assistant coach, Joe Wooten. I remember that they were so casual, eating their sandwiches and wearing sweat suits and not saying much. I was turned off by that, thinking, I am the number one recruit in the nation, they are supposed to try to pursue me, and show me around the school, but they seemed unimpressed, and I was turned off by that.

I also had other high school coaches from around DC calling me and encouraging me to come to their schools. Some of these were loosely run Christian academies which had top basketball programs but were light on academics. I knew I need a good academic program since I had a dream of attending Duke. It was something I thought about nearly every day. Duke.

I had already received recruiting mail from Duke, so I knew I was on their radar. I had a lucky day that summer that led me to a recruiting trip to Duke. I was working out at the Boys & Girls Club like I normally did, and this girl named Janae Hayes saw me playing. Janae was from my area, and she was a rising senior at Duke, and a member of the women's basketball team. She watched me in the gym and was really impressed. She called Jason Williams and Nate James right then and told them about me. A few days later, I was on an unofficial visit to Duke. I rode down to North Carolina with Janae and got to play a few of the Duke players one on one. They discovered I was tough to guard, even as an eighth grader and they were having some fun and laughing when they couldn't catch me. That visit sparked my dream and I knew Duke was for me. I knew what college I wanted to attend before I knew where I wanted to go to high school.

Earl was a ninth grader at Gonzaga, so I had heard all about his experiences there every night when we talked. Then one night we had a big conversation.

"Where are you going to go?" Earl asked.

"I don't know, DeMatha is the best, I should go there, but I don't know."

"Don't go to DeMatha," Earl said, "You know what

man, you are my little brother, let's do this. Let's go all the way to the pros together. I want you to play with me at Gonzaga!"

Earl and I were competitive with each other. But this was one of those times when Earl really came forward, and I was like man, my brother really wants us to do this together. So, I was in. I called the next day and said, I'm going to Gonzaga.

Chapter Six

Being thirteen years old can be confusing enough, but in the summer of 2000, I was simultaneously feeling like I was on top of the world, but also worried that I was going to be dethroned at any minute. I felt like I had good people on my side, but I knew that I had wronged an important mentor in my life, and I didn't know how to handle that. I was also faced with starting high school, and not just any high school, but one of the most prestigious and rigorous private schools in DC. And I was entering this school at only 13 years old, making me the youngest student at Gonzaga College High School.

Summer time was always pretty wild at Sursum Corda. It was party time, and all the kids were out a lot and usually that was when they got into trouble. I wasn't one to get mixed up with drugs or any type of trouble because I saw a future for myself. I was busy at the Club, spending time in the gym at Gonzaga, or traveling to games with Rob and the Blue Devils. I was so busy with practices and traveling, that I was, at times, very separate from what was going on at Sursum Corda. I was away physically, but I was also distant in my mindset, because I had goals for myself. I was a very driven and disciplined child, so I stayed away from drugs and hustling. Some of my friends started to slip into drug abuse that summer, but I didn't really get to feel it. It was all at a distance for me. I was watching it and aware of it, but it didn't involve me.

But even if I had wanted to get into that world, it never would have been allowed. The gangsters at Sursum Corda wouldn't let me near any of it. Not only was I not allowed to smoke weed or make some money selling drugs, they would send me back into my house whenever there was a fight or police activity. They were proud of me, and they wanted to see me succeed. Our neighborhood was tight, people looked out for each other and protected each other.

I didn't need to sell drugs. Let's face it, the reason people sell drugs is for money. But I was affiliated with Nike from the time I was 10 years old, so I always had what I needed. I was a certified Nike tester, so I got several shipments a year of sneakers and gear. I filled out questionnaires on new shoes they were considering bringing to market, and I rated the durability and the look.

I remember a couple times the delivery truck came and men loaded the boxes of gear into my house, and the gangsters would come by and say, "Whatever you don't want, Toe, just bring it on out." And I would give them a lot of it, all for free.

There was a guy in the neighborhood who we called Frank Nitti, or just Nitti. He was named after Al

Capone's enforcer. Nitti was a tough guy who was said to be the enforcer for the leaders at Sursum Corda. But he was also a guy who showed a lot of interest in me and acted protective toward me. I often gave him sneakers or shirts when my Nike shipment came in.

The sneaker companies also gave me money; envelopes of cash delivered through a friend, something that I didn't know was unethical. When you are thirteen and someone hands you an envelope with a few hundred dollars, you take it!

Early in the summer, Curtis Malone was sniffing around looking for me. He was the coach of DC Assault, the Adidas youth team that Earl had joined. I was with a Nike team, and I had only gone to Nike tournaments up until this time, so I hadn't seen Curtis at any tournaments. When I heard he was looking for me, I knew exactly what he wanted. It was a recruiting visit, and Coach Rob had warned me it was going to happen. I finally let him approach me since I knew it was inevitable.

Now Curtis doesn't look like a typical basketball coach, he was more of a street guy. He was a real likeable guy, a salesman, and his stock at Adidas rose real quick.

Curtis came up to me and was logical about it. "Man, you are the number one 8th grade player on the Nike circuit. Sebastian Telfair is the number one guy on the Adidas circuit. You will never get to go against each other and see who really has that number one spot until you are able to play each other. The world wants to see you two go head to head. The media will cover this, the college coaches will notice, it will be big. But the only way you can do this is if you join my team. Come over to Adidas, it's better for you."

Every kid on the summer circuit had the goal of being invited to a big select tournament. It was either the Nike All American Camp or the Adidas ABCD tournament. Curtis told me he would guarantee that I would go to the ABCD tournament that summer, where I would probably be the youngest by several years and I could match up against the best 17 and 18-year olds in the country. He said that Sebastian and I would both be invited, and we would make headlines as the youngest players to ever be invited to a major summer event.

To me as a competitor, I just took that as something important and it got me to switch really quick since I knew I could get that exposure I wanted. At that time, the word on the street was that the Adidas players were better. With the older guys, Luol Deng was ranked second in the nation, and LeBron James was number one. Luol was on the Nike circuit, but LeBron was on Adidas and he was the true number one. I saw it as Adidas being a number one place, a circuit for the winners.

I wanted to be a winner. I wanted to find the highest level of competition that I could. I told Curtis I would join DC Assault. I chose not to think about the fact that I was quitting on Rob, and in fact, I decided I wouldn't even tell him.

Within a week, I was on a plane to Los Angeles with the DC Assault team. I never called Rob to tell him, I just decided to avoid the whole confrontation. But it did weigh on me.

Traveling with Curtis was a lot of fun, he didn't have same rules or decorum that I was used to with the Blue Devils. He wasn't on us about anything, we could even wear our uniform shirts untucked, and he didn't seem to care about what we did. One thing that really surprised me was that two of the older guys, about 17 and 18 years old, had brought their girlfriends along on the trip. Apparently, Adidas paid for a hotel room for these young couples and their airfare, but I'm not sure if the higher ups at Adidas knew about this. But with Curtis, it was ok.

Our first stop was the Adidas Big Time Tournament in LA. We did pretty well, but what I remember most was a visit to Sonny Vaccaro's house. Sonny was a youth basketball legend. He was an Adidas corporate guy, the founder of the ABCD tournament and the national high school all-American tournament. He knew all the big-time players. He even knew Michael Jordan since Sonny was the one who signed him to his first sneaker deal. It was just a few of us who got to go to Sonny's house. There were three or four of us from DC Assault, but he also had other kids from youth teams from other parts of the country who were in town for the LA tournament. We got to swim in his pool, and we met his wife too.

I had a private workout on the basketball court at Sonny's house with Kiki Vandeweghe. He was a major NBA player before my time, and at this point he was coaching and doing on-air analysis with ESPN. I don't know why I was picked for this workout, but I knew it was a big deal and it made me feel like maybe I would make it to the NBA. Vandeweghe became the head coach of the Denver Nuggets soon after our time at Sonny's house, and he is now working in basketball operations with the NBA.

Sonny took me and a couple of the guys into his basement which was like a giant warehouse of Adidas gear. He had boxes and boxes of everything from sneakers to headbands, jerseys, and bags. "You can all take as much as you can carry," he said, "Take whatever you want. But remember this: If you want to be successful in basketball, stay with Adidas."

The most memorable thing about that west coast trip was when I snuck out of the hotel room at night to go to the beach with a couple of the guys. We went around the corner toward the pool and we all smelled something familiar. The smell of weed was in the air. The other guys started to go back, but I kept going around the corner and there I could see Curtis and all of our other coaches sitting by the pool smoking. I was shocked! I ran back to the guys saying incredulously, "Our coaches smoke weed! Our coaches smoke weed!" We all started to laugh and ran back to the hotel room.

When I got back from LA, I started hiding from Rob. My mom told me that he had called her as soon as he heard the news from the basketball media that I was out in LA, playing with DC Assault in the Adidas Big Time Tournament.

My mom didn't get involved in the analytics of basketball, all she wanted to know was that everything was going to be taken care of. She didn't want to dish out any money for any of these trips. She also didn't want me to miss school. She knew that I had a great relationship with Rob, and that spending time with him was good for me. But she also knew Curtis from my brother being on his team, and he is such a salesman, I'm sure he was nice to my mom. When it came to this, where I was leaving Rob to go to Curtis and causing a big feud, I know she was a little shaken up by it. I think she was questioning my decision. She told me that I was going to let Rob down. She knew that Rob was going to be hurt about it.

I hid from Rob for about a week after I got back. I didn't know what to tell him. I wasn't ready to tell him. I would ignore his phone calls and hide out if I saw his car come into Sursum Corda.

Finally, he caught up with me when he came by my house and he just looked at me and said, "Man, what's up?"

He talked to me for a while and said that I needed to understand who is loyal to me and who has my best interests at heart. Bad influences can steer me wrong. "I have been loyal to you, Eric. The thing about this future in basketball is that you have to know who has good intentions for you. Who is looking out for you? Who is using you. I told you this was going to come up, and I told you to prepare for it, and here it is."

But the thing about me being only thirteen years old is that I didn't understand the complexities of the whole situation. I wanted to be the best player I could be. Curtis baited me with an opportunity to challenge Sebastian Telfair, and he knew just what to say. I don't think my brain was even ready to understand this type of thing at this age. I was impulsive, I looked at things in a black and white way. I didn't treat Rob the way I should have.

And it couldn't have happened to a better guy. Rob was one of the major positive influences on my life. He didn't just want the best players, he wanted structure and good team values. That is why we were so hard to beat because we had good coaching, we worked together, and everyone knew his role. Rob was always on me, and he got on me when I was wrong, and he praised me when I was right. He taught me restaurant eating etiquette, how to say please and thank you, how to wear my uniform properly. What he taught me was everything to me. Even now, I think back to many of those lessons about how to act and how to present yourself when I'm meeting with people or going to an interview.

His lessons and influence resonated with me over the years. But unfortunately, at age thirteen, I wasn't hearing any of it and I didn't treat the man the way he deserved to be treated. I stayed with Curtis Malone and DC Assault for some time and ignited a feud between him and Rob Jackson that went on for years.

Chapter Seven

My tenure at Gonzaga started a few months before freshman orientation. Summer league was a big thing in the DC basketball community, and it was my first chance to play my game so close to home. Summer league started in early June, just a few days after I had graduated from eighth grade.

I was a ball of nerves about the whole thing. I had lots of sleepless nights, because of the competitiveness in me. Although I knew I was good enough in my head, I wondered, would I make the team? Would I have to play JV? Can I be the best defensive player on this team as a freshman? I was ranked as the number one guard in the country, recruited by Duke and a hundred other colleges, but what if I go to tryouts and I don't even make it? What if they take me on varsity but they never play me? Those thoughts were horrifying to me. I talked to my mom, my brother, and a few coaches about it. I really wanted to quit Gonzaga if I didn't make varsity and transfer to one of the Christian academies that were recruiting me so hard. Finding this possible way out for myself would calm me down for a moment, then I would go back to being nervous about it again. I wouldn't know whether I made varsity until November, so I had several months to sweat it out. First, I had to get through summer league.

Earl and I went up to the gym on the first day of summer league practice. I was pretty revved up about it. There were three other rising freshmen there, but there were also several new Gonzaga graduates who were on their way to college. They would play in the summer league one last time before joining their college teams.

I saw Howard Blue as soon as I walked in; he was talking and laughing with a group of guys. At 6'8 and 260 pounds, he was a big man who had dominated in the WCAC (Washington Catholic Athletic Conference), now on his way to Colgate University.

Guys used to say, "Stay away from Big Howard in the paint!" He was so imposing, that players usually took a shot from outside rather than going up against him with a layup.

I ended up getting into a fight with Howard that day, which wasn't the best start to my career at Gonzaga.

Because I went into the practice under so much pressure, I was feeling really aggressive. I knew I had to prepare mentally and physically for a transition which would not be seamless. I had to prove myself. I was starting all over, in a way. Not only was I in ninth grade but I was also one of the youngest in the class. Outwardly, I acted like I was so sure of myself, but inside, I was not feeling confident.

During practice, Howard fouled me hard, maybe intentional, maybe not, but it was a play and all within the confines of the game. Maybe he did it since I had been acting so cocky, this little kid coming to the varsity team acting like he owned the place. I went up for a layup and he slammed me down. It didn't hurt me physically as much as it hurt my pride. I was 6 feet tall, but only about 130 pounds, so to go up against a guy Howard's size was tough. He knocked me out of the air and I fell hard.

At the time, I was thinking I had something to prove. I didn't care that these guys are in high school, I had been playing older guys for years. I just came from an Adidas trip where I was guarding JJ Reddick, who was going to Duke, and now I am going to get shown up by Howard Blue, going to Colgate? No way. I went into the practice trying to prove to everyone that I was going to make an impact on that team. I can't be outdone by a guy going to Colgate since I am supposed to be this big bad DI player. I was infuriated.

With that fight, I felt like I had something to prove. Me being the neighborhood guy, coming from Sursum Corda, I knew I had to prove myself on day one, that is the way of the streets. I lashed out quickly.

After Howard knocked me down, I was screaming and cursing. "I'm gunna get a gun! I'm coming back and going to get you all!" I yelled as I stormed out of the gym.

How I grew up, guns were accessible and when a

fight broke out and things were escalating, that is what you would do. I was going to get a gun. Being around that for so long, it just made me do the same thing, and since I felt threatened, that was how I reacted.

I ran out of that gym, screaming threats. The coaches tried to stop me, but I was out of there. By the time I ran the 500 yards to Sursum Corda, the guys on the corner saw I was upset and came to help. They were ready to get a gun, ready to help me out, when just as quickly my mom opened the door from our house and called me inside. She gave me a hug and told me it would be okay. Earl was right behind me. We had a moment where my mom got the whole story from both of us.

"Earl, you go on back to practice and tell Coach Whitaker everything is ok. Toe is going to stay home today, but he'll be back tomorrow. Tell him there is going to be no trouble."

And when I went back the next day, Howard came right over to me and gave me a high five. "Welcome back," he said. We never had a problem again. Howard is a man who I came to admire greatly over the years. After graduating from Colgate, he became the athletic director at the Washington Jesuit Academy, a middle school for boys from low income communities, that Coach Whitaker went on to start about a year or two after this incident.

I also had a long talk with Coach Whitaker that day, about what was acceptable and what was not. We ended up having talks almost every day that I was at Gonzaga. We talked about how to treat people, how to react to situations, how to plan your day, and just about every other detail of life you can imagine. Coach Whitaker was always fired up, full of enthusiasm, and he expected so much from his players, both in basketball, but also in academics and personal life. That's how it is at a Jesuit school, it's about the whole person. Coach Whitaker believed in me and that meant a lot to me at the time.

Up until that point in my life, I made mistakes and acted impulsively. There were things that I did wrong that I wasn't corrected about. I got away with a lot. And I lived in an environment where problems were solved with violence. But the people at Gonzaga really helped me. They know boys and they are committed to developing the whole person. I always wish I had stayed longer at Gonzaga.

Chapter Eight

My college recruiting mail had been piling up all summer, and Coach Whitaker promised I could look at it on the first day of school. NCAA recruiting regulations didn't allow coaches to contact athletes directly, so they sent my mail in care of my high school coach. Some colleges sent several letters a week, so my pile of mail grew big enough to fill a small crate from the post office.

I had a great first day at Gonzaga, and I felt just as welcomed as I had at Holy Trinity. My best friend Morris was a fellow freshman, as were five or six boys from our eighth-grade class. I kept thinking about my recruiting letters as I went from one class to the other. Then when I was finally done, I headed over to Coach Whitaker's office to see the bin full of mail.

"Hi Eric, how was your first day?" Coach Whitaker greeted me.

"Good," I said, glancing around the room until I saw the mail crate behind his desk.

Coach Whitaker smiled and knew what I was looking for. "Let's meet once a week to go through the mail," he proposed, "We can have a talk, look at the letters and do some research on the colleges."

"OK, but can I take my mail home today?" I asked.

"You can take five letters home. The rest can stay here."

I bent down to the floor and started to dig through the mail. I saw Notre Dame, Illinois, UCLA, and Memphis. I started frantically sifting through the letters until I found one from Duke.

"Ahhh!" I said, ripping it open, "Duke! Yes!"

The letter was signed by Coach K, so I picked it to take with me that day, and I kept it for many years. I also took letters from UCLA and Stanford. I saw a letter from Harvard, so I took that one, feeling flattered to be recruited by a brainy school like Harvard, even though I knew I would never consider going there. At home, I taped the letters to the wall in my room and looked at them every day.

My brother Earl started tenth grade at Gonzaga, but he left before basketball season started. Curtis Malone had been chirping in his ear about how unnecessary all that homework at Gonzaga was.

"Why are you doing all that? They have you doing two hours of homework a night! You don't need that, man" Curtis said, exasperated. "What do you need that for?"

"I don't know," Earl agreed, "It's all so hard."

"Listen to me, all you need to do is qualify. You qualify through the NCAA clearinghouse by getting the score you need on the SAT and taking certain credits. You are fine with that. You can't play basketball at this level and be worrying about two hours of homework every day!"

It was easy to agree with him. We were young and impressionable, and an adult was telling us that we were doing more homework and were under more academic pressure than we needed to be. Earl and I both became influenced by this point of view.

Curtis had issues with the coaching staff at Gonzaga. He frequently drove to Gonzaga to pick up Earl for DC Assault practice, only to be told that Earl had study hall, or Earl was in the weight room, or having an unofficial practice in the gym. "He's gotta go," Curtis would say, "I have to get him to practice."

One day Coach Whitaker and Coach Turner went up to him at the gym entrance and told him that only a parent could come into the school and take a student out of his scheduled after-school activity.

Things got heated and Curtis insisted that he would come and get his player whenever he wanted. "It's none of your business!" he yelled at Coach Turner.

This resulted in Curtis Malone being banned from Gonzaga's campus.

Curtis started talking about getting Earl out of Gonzaga permanently. Coach Whitaker and Coach Turner talked to Earl about getting his grades up, meeting with a tutor, going for extra help, or coming to after-school study hall. The two camps had decidedly different opinions on what Earl should do.

But for Earl, it was an easy decision. He had never liked studying and the work at Gonzaga was getting harder and harder. He was on academic probation and would not be able to play unless he got his grades up quickly. Also, Curtis had the ear of so many top college coaches, and he was confident and convincing in his opinion about keeping the academics light. Curtis was essentially telling Earl that he was a fool for playing by Gonzaga's rules.

It was decided that Earl would leave Gonzaga and join the tenth-grade class at New Hampton School, a boarding school in New Hampshire. Curtis had a connection there and talked to the basketball coach about Earl. The Georgetown tutors, who had a scholarship fund for Sursum Corda kids, vetted the school and provided a small amount toward tuition and a plane ticket for Earl. New Hampton School awarded him a scholarship for the rest of the tuition.

Going to boarding school was starting to be a popular thing for high school basketball players. It had all worked out for our local idol, DerMarr Johnson. He was Curtis' launching pad into high stakes youth basketball. At the time Earl was making this decision, DerMarr had just signed a big contract with the NBA's Atlanta Hawks, at only twenty years old. It was Curtis who discovered him at age 14, and Curtis who had moved him to two different private schools, including a boarding school called Maine Central Institute.

New Yorker magazine had called teenaged DerMarr, "Magic Johnson with a jump shot" and "the next Penny Hardaway." There was talk about DerMarr going right to the NBA after high school, but some scouts were saying he wasn't ready, and they cast doubt on whether this was the right move. It was Curtis who guided DerMarr and his mother through all the changes and decisions, which ultimately resulted in him signing a contract with the Atlanta Hawks after just one year of college ball at the University of Cincinnati.

My mother thought it was a smart idea to get Earl to boarding school and out of our neighborhood. She knew it had worked out so well for other young players, and she wouldn't have to worry about his safety up in New Hampshire. While Maine Central, and some of the other schools that young basketball prospects went to were not much more than basketball and SAT prep boot camps, New Hampton was a real school. It offered an International Baccalaureate diploma and had students from all over the world.

Earl left for New Hampton, and I went on to basketball tryouts at Gonzaga without him. I was still nervous about making the team, and with all the talk of changing schools, I had it in the back of my mind that I would leave Gonzaga if I didn't make varsity.

On the last day of tryouts, the coaches told us that the team would be posted outside the office in the morning. I ran up there first thing in the morning, once the doors were opened. The other boys were there too, and it was chaotic with more the fifty boys checking the results.

I pushed through the crowd, making some guys push me back or frown at me. I walked over the Gonzaga school seal which I was not supposed to step on, out of respect for the school. But I had forgotten, in my desperation to get to that list. I scrolled down, looked at all the names, saw mine, and yelled, "Yes!"

I made varsity. Three other freshmen also made the team that year, but since I was still thirteen, I was the youngest. Some people told me I was the youngest boy to ever play Gonzaga varsity basketball. I was surprised that a neighborhood friend named Lorenzo Miles, who was a sophomore, was put on junior varsity. He was a friend of Earl's and for most of my childhood, I was trying to keep up with the two of them, and now to see that I made varsity and he didn't, both surprised me and gave me a feeling that I was really moving forward with my game. I was excited about the upcoming season and ready to make an impact.

"HE'S A FRESHMAN!" the Gonzaga boys chanted from the stands when I was on the court. If I had a great shot, or got past a defender, they let loose with "HE'S A FRESHMAN!" chant and it always made me smile. Guys would high five me in the hallways, ask me to sit with them at lunch, and they loved to talk basketball with me.

I was named starting point guard, taking over the

role from my brother Earl after his transfer. Our season was off to a strong start with a 5-1 record when we flew to Dallas for a tournament. It was a bonding experience and our team got close.

I made good friends on the team, but Morris was still my best friend. He and I stuck to our usual routine of doing homework together, discussing the best ways to study, and motivating each other. Morris didn't have a big thing in his life like basketball, so he had to fight the pull of the streets every day.

I connected with a math teacher named Paul Buckley. Mr. Buckley had graduated from Gonzaga himself, about fifteen years before I got there, so he was a young teacher, full of enthusiasm and encouragement. I often met Mr. Buckley for extra help and some conversation about life. I had found my mentors at Gonzaga: Coaches Whitaker and Turner, and Mr. Buckley the math teacher. They were my team, and I knew they were working as hard toward my success as I was. Many years later, when I had my first job as a high school math teacher, Paul Buckley met with me, shared his lesson plans and helped me create my own lessons plans.

Gonzaga hosted its annual DC Classic basketball tournament which had four local teams, including our rivals, Georgetown Prep and Good Counsel, along with four teams from out of state. Strake Jesuit came from Houston, St Joseph's from Philadelphia, both known to be strong competitors. We won a tough semi-final game against Georgetown Prep before a crowd of hundreds. Antwan Harrison, a fellow freshman, and I dominated in that game. We met Good Counsel in the finals and were behind the entire first half. But we roared from behind and took the game to overtime. Feeling our best under pressure, we pulled off the tournament win.

We played in the Alhambra Classic in Maryland, which was a tournament for Catholic schools, such as DeMatha and Roman Catholic of Philadelphia. On the first day, we played Towson Catholic which had 6'5 swingman Carmelo Anthony. He had been making a name for himself, so I was ready to do my best to shut him down. Gonzaga beat Towson Catholic 54-47 and we went on to win the whole tournament. Carmelo ended up transferring to a boarding program called Oak Hill and his star rose from there. He played a year at Syracuse where he led them to the NCAA tournament title, then went on to be one of the top players in the NBA.

Next up was a memorable tournament called the Vistar Classic in Roanoke, Virginia. I knew that we would be playing Cave Spring High School, led by J.J. Reddick. I was still obsessed with Duke, and it was all over the media that junior J.J. Reddick had just committed to Coach K and the Blue Devils. I went into that tournament focused on playing my best against Reddick and taking every opportunity I could to dominate him. I knew that Duke coaches would be watching, so I was ready to play for the win.

We started off strong and led the entire game. I focused all my attention on guarding J.J. and trying to keep him from taking a shot. He was a prolific scorer and a three-point pro. He routinely scored twenty or thirty points a game and had netted 43 points in the Virginia state championship game. I played like I was on fire that day and went after everything I could. But Cave Spring came back hard and won 72-64, with Reddick scoring 29 points. I gave him a high five at the end and was hopeful that I would soon see him at Duke.

After basketball season ended, it was harder for me to keep my grades up. The team study halls and meetings had ended and the coaches, while still checking in on me, did so less frequently. I started my spring practices with DC Assault and Curtis Malone, so I heard opinions on how Gonzaga was too much work, too many rules, too restrictive.

The problem with Curtis' opinion was that it didn't work out so well for Earl at New Hampton. From a basketball point of view, he started at point guard and had a great season. Rashad McCants from North Carolina was a team mate and friend. Rashad went on to be an honor roll student at New Hampton while also being named McDonald's All American and New Hampshire Player of the Year before signing with University of North Carolina, and ultimately going on to a long career in the NBA. Earl liked the coach, the guys on the team, and everything about the basketball program.

It was the rules of boarding school life that got to Earl. He wasn't used to being told where to be at all times and he didn't like being monitored. Academically, he found that there was even less structure than he had at Gonzaga. At New Hampton, they offered helped if needed, but no one was requiring Earl to go to study hall or to finish his English paper. It was a lot of small infractions and then a marijuana incident, and finally a conflict with some hockey players, that made New Hampton decide that it wasn't the right place for Earl. He came home in April, just in time to start spring practices with DC Assault. He enrolled at Dunbar High to finish out the year while he looked for a new school.

I told Mr. Buckley about Earl getting kicked out of New Hampton, and he offered to tutor Earl so that he would pass the year at Dunbar. He also started checking in with me more often on my academic progress at Gonzaga.

"It's not all about basketball you know" Mr. Buckley said to me one day, "You can't get consumed by it."

"I know," I answered, "I do have other things I like to do."

"Really? Like what"

I thought of my time at church, singing in the choir, and fun times with my friends when we wrote rap songs, performed routines and songs for our friends. "I like to sing," I answered.

Mr. Buckley asked me about my interest in singing.

Then he suggested something, "Why don't you try out for the school play?"

"No way, "I said,

"Come on, try something new." Mr. Buckley said.

"What play is it?"

"It's Hello Dolly," he stated as I smirked, "You should do it. You really should."

And would you believe that I did try out for Hello Dolly and I got a small role? I went to the practices and enjoyed the feeling of being in a big production with sets, costumes, and a group of kids that were preparing for the show as a team. On the night of the show, I was so proud to see both Mr. Buckley and Coach Whitaker in the audience. They came up to me after the performance to congratulate me, and it made me feel like they really cared about me as a person, not just as a basketball player.

But the pull of the basketball world came hard at the end of the school year. My grades had slipped terribly. Morris had started to get into drugs and he started hanging out in the street at night. Earl was also slipping into that world. It was hard to watch and made me feel very unsettled. Morris had changed, he wasn't himself, and it seemed like he had become addicted. He did go back to Gonzaga for tenth grade, but he was kicked out after he was caught selling drugs on campus. He lived the street life for a few more years before killing someone in a fight and getting charged with murder. He ended up beating the charge since it was ruled self-defense, but he still spent most of his late teens and twenties in prison on drug charges. Morris had been such a strong student, so well-liked by everyone at Holy Trinity and Gonzaga, it was hard to see him go down this path.

Curtis Malone pushed hard for me to leave Gonzaga and find a new school. Because he was banned from campus, he had no access to me and he continued to reason that the school work was too hard and too risky for a player who only needed to qualify. And finally came another big issue: our coaches asked the team to play only Gonzaga summer league. No AAU tournament, no Big Time in Las Vegas, no ABCD tournament, they were asking us to simply stay in DC and play summer league.

"There's no way I'm doing that," I said to Coach Whitaker, "I'm invited to all the big tournaments this summer."

Coach Whitaker nodded, "But why do you need that? You have a crate full of college recruiting letters. Duke is interested in you, just as you want. All you need to do is stay on track and we can help you do that right here."

"But I have to keep up my ranking, I have to play with the good guys. And I like going to tournaments."

"We've talked to the coaches at Duke on your behalf. They won't change their opinion if you miss the tournaments. Your challenge is more about keeping your grades up and keeping bad influences away. We can help you do that here. You had a successful year, think of what you can do if you stay here until you graduate."

Later that day, I talked to Rob Jackson. He was still very much in my life, even though I was playing for DC Assault. There were times when I floated between both teams, attending Rob's practices and Curtis's in the same week, and sometimes playing Blue Devils tournaments.

Rob was firm in his opinion, "In order to get better, you have to play at a higher level. I'm not sure Gonzaga summer league is going to let you do that. If you want to reach your goals in basketball, you have to get out there and challenge yourself and play against the best players in the country. You have to go to the summer tournaments."

I agreed with him. I decided to leave Gonzaga.

Coach Whitaker invited me and my mom to come to meet with him on the last day of school. He was sad that I was leaving, and he wanted us both to know he would always help me in whatever way he could. I got the sense that he felt things were about to get difficult for me. I saw the concern on his face.

Coach Whitaker was a guy who believed in empowering young people and helping them to do well in all aspects of their lives. About a year after I left Gonzaga, Whitaker left too. He became the headmaster of a new school called the Washington Jesuit Academy, a middle school for low income boys which offers an extended day, summer program, and lots of support and guidance. He has been working there ever since, inspiring boys and helping them to reach their goals in life.

That day, Coach Whitaker said that I could finally take my mail crate of college recruiting letters home with me.

I said thank you, gave him a hug, and walked out the door and into the rain with my mom, trying to keep my college recruiting mail from getting wet. It was tough to leave. I knew I was giving up all the support and positive influences that had been so helpful to me. But I was extremely driven to play basketball at the highest level and to do what I could to advance myself. I was going down the rabbit hole and excited to see what was next.

Chapter Nine

I started off the summer taking a trip to New York with Eddie Lau. He was a guy who I knew from basketball tournaments. He was friendly, always around, and the coaches and players seemed to know him. I heard that he was a sports agent, or some kind of deal maker, but I wasn't sure who he worked with or exactly what he did. Curtis knew him and had vouched for him, so when he invited me to New York, I was game.

He picked me up in a Cadillac Escalade and we drove first to New Jersey, to pick up a kid name Derrick Caracter. Derrick was fourteen like, me but 6'9 and 285 pounds, which got him lots of attention from the media and invitations to all the summer tournaments. There was talk that Derrick was the next Shaq.

I didn't know exactly who Eddie was or why I was in New York, but I had a great trip. We went to Brooklyn to watch the practice of an AAU team called the NY Gauchos. Its star was Sebastian Telfair, and he seemed to know Eddie too. We went out for dinner, looked around New York, and Derrick and I stayed in our own room in a hotel.

Later, I did some research and found that Eddie

Lau was a registered agent and a runner for a well-known basketball agent named Dan Fegan. I realized later that Fegan was DerMarr Johnson's agent, and he got this role after Curtis told DerMarr which agent to pick. Eddie treated us to a fun weekend in New York and never asked us to work with him in the future, and he never said anything about what he did for a living.

Back at home, there was some push and pull between Rob Jackson and Curtis Malone. I was still going back and forth between both teams. I had a connection with Rob, I knew I could trust him. But Curtis was more glamour and glitz and excitement, and I ended up staying on DC Assault with him.

It makes you wonder how a convicted crack cocaine drug dealer could even coach a youth sport, with all the background checks and screenings that were required. The Washington Post had a story about Curtis' past convictions, but it didn't stop him. His empire grew and grew with more teams added, more staff, and more connections with college coaches. He started out with a $50,000 annual salary from Adidas, but by the end he was getting a half million a year to support DC Assault programs. Of course, a lot of that went to pay assistant coaches, so Curtis wasn't getting it all, but he was well compensated. He had at least one NBA player who paid him a monthly salary in gratitude for his help in the past. Curtis was successful, and so many guys said that it was Curtis Malone who changed their lives and helped them to get places that they never could have made it to on their own.

Curtis's strategy for success was to get talent. You needed the talent to get the exposure, and then it built on itself as talented players were drawn to DC Assault. Colleges coaches said that you couldn't recruit in DC without going through Curtis Malone. He worked with Duke's Coach K, and Billy Donovan, Bob Huggins and just about every major college coach.

It was only Gary Williams from University of Maryland who refused to work with Malone saying, "I know what he is," to the Washington Post in an interview.

Rob Jackson was quoted in Sports Illustrated saying of Curtis Malone, "I ran my program as an amateur program. He ran his as a business. He sold kids to schools, sold kids to agents."

I was still talking to Rob and going to some Blue Devils practices, but I officially played on the DC Assault team in the summer of 2001. We flew to tournaments in Las Vegas and Los Angeles, before ending the summer at the ABCD tournament in New Jersey. It was the marque event for the summer basketball circuit and all the major college coaches were there. Sebastian Telfair, Derrick Caracter and I were among the youngest invited to the event, and we all played strong and got a lot of attention. My brother Earl made it to the tournament too.

The players at ABCD went to classes and listened

to guest speakers who gave us an insight into future careers in basketball. Kobe Bryant talked to us, and I remember feeling inspired and impressed with him. There was a bus that took us from the hotel to the tournament site. But there were two guys who never went by bus. A limo came to pick them up. It was my nemesis, Sebastian Telfair, and a guy named Lenny Cooke. They were the "it" guys of the tournament, who got all the attention. The girl rapper, Foxy Brown, was in the stands watching, and when she got into the limo with Lenny and Sebastian, we all went crazy. The tournament was supposed to be about basketball and preparation for college, but it was also quite a spectacle.

The summer of 2001 was the year of Lenny Cooke. He was rated higher than LeBron James or any player and he had a camera crew following him filming a documentary. But it was a game at the camp, where LeBron and Lenny went one-on-one, that got a lot of attention. LeBron outscored Lenny 21-9 in the game and finished him off with an incredible shot where he kicked his feet back and seemed to be airborne, floating toward the basket and getting nothing but net. The crowd roared, and symbolically, that was the beginning of the end for Lenny. He had bad advice and poor grades and didn't advance as he hoped. But that day at ABCD camp, before LeBron dominated him, he got to ride in the limo with Foxy Brown while LeBron and the rest of us were on the bus.

Earl and I were both named to the Underclassman

All Star team. It was a big honor and we got to play a game in front of all the college coaches and members of the media at the tournament.

I had to go head-to-hear with my rival, Sebastian Telfair from Brooklyn. He was fast and smart, but I came out strong, and I scored the first six points of the game. But then I jumped for a three-point shot and came down awkwardly on the guy who was defending me, and my foot twisted. I came out of the game to ice it. It was swollen, and they made me sit out the rest of the game. But still, my prospects rose after that tournament, and I started to get even more recruiting mail and attention in the basketball media. I was feeling confident about my game and prospects for the future.

The decision of which high school to attend was an easier one the second time around. I was purely focused on basketball, and I chose a nationally-ranked program, Montrose Christian, which was ranked number 18 in the USA Today top basketball teams in the country. It was known to have one of the best coaches in high school basketball, Stu Vetter. I knew that my game would get better by attending Montrose.

Coach Vetter had been the architect of several other nationally ranked programs at tiny private schools. He was a nomadic coach, bringing his coaching skills, Nike sponsorship, and recruited players to a small school, becoming a basketball powerhouse, then moving on to another school and doing the same thing. He was that good. Named one of the most "winningest" coaches in high school basketball, he was known to be a high-level coach who helped players get to the next level. He had been at Montrose for just a year when I joined, and he was already off to a great start.

Montrose Christian was a K-12 school with fewer than 200 students, located in Rockville, Maryland. There were about 25 students in each grade in high school, so it was tiny. But this gave Coach Vetter the opportunity to recruit students and run a professional style basketball program. We were not restricted by the rules of a public school or more traditional private school. We could get our work done and focus on what we needed to do on the basketball court. One NBA player and Montrose graduate, Terrance Ross, reflected fondly on the school in a Washington Post article, adding, "It was more like a basketball academy with a school." After the rigorous academic program at Gonzaga, this was just what I was looking for.

I decided to repeat my freshman year, which we called "re-classifying." I still moved forward in some of my classes, so I wasn't exactly repeating the same thing. I took Algebra I in my ninth-grade year at Gonzaga and moved on to take Geometry in my second ninth grade year at Montrose. This change put me with my peers. I started ninth grade at Montrose at age fourteen, and I turned fifteen at the end of December, which is a typical age for a freshman. This move would be better for college recruiting and al better for succeeding at college, since I was now on path to go to college at 18, which is the norm, rather than the young age of 17.

There were four other freshmen on the basketball team and I became good friends with Mike Freeman and Ryan Scott. Ryan's father, Dennis Scott, was an NBA player who had played for Stu Vetter in high school. Now he had enrolled his son Ryan at Montrose so that he could play for Coach Vetter too.

When basketball season started, the commute from DC to Rockville got long, so I spent most nights at the houses of my two friends, who lived close to the school. One time, I was at Ryan Scott's house and his father had his former Orlando Magic teammate, Shaquille O'Neal over. I was excited to meet Shaq, but I also found myself to be almost mute. Shaq was so huge, such a presence, and had this great sense of humor, that it made me feel intimidated. He was larger than life, and one of the most interesting people I have ever met.

I liked my daily life at Montrose because it was a small and friendly school. I was elected president of the freshman class and got good grades. But my focus was basketball. It was a whole new level of basketball, which seemed very professional. For the first time in my life, I was studying the game, everything from technique and mechanics, to game strategy, and the simple method of practicing certain things repetitively.

Stu Vetter was an amazing teacher of the game. He was a coach like no other, and he taught us how to improve. He knew the mechanics of the game and could correct a shooting style or teach us a play in a way that helped the whole team maximize the game.

Coach Vetter always said, "Luck is when opportunity meets preparation." We practiced drills over and over again. We were on that court so many hours that things grew instinctive and we were able to execute at a high-level during games.

He was a strict coach, but we also had fun. One time, we were tied 88-88 and Coach Vetter had me sit on the end of the bench, so it looked like I was waiting to go in. We only had four on the court and me on the bench, but just for a few seconds, and they didn't notice. Then the ball moved, I jumped in from the bench and scored the game winning basket.

College coaches were in our gym all the time. I saw Coach K, John Calipari, and Tubby Smith at more than one of our practices. Coach Vetter had good relationships with so many of the college coaches. He would always say to the kids who didn't get much playing time, that his connections were good, and he would do the best he could at vouching for all his players and getting them spots in college programs.

The Montrose Christian basketball program was hard work, so many hours of basketball, but also it involved a lot of time on the road. In order to maintain our national high school ranking, we had to travel. I got to go on the most exciting trip of my life that year. We were scheduled to play in the Iolani Classic in Hawaii and Coach Vetter let us spend ten days there. We had plenty of time at the beach, some sight-seeing, and bonding as a team. For me, it was the trip of a lifetime.

Earl also decided to repeat a grade and "reclassify" when he joined the sophomore class at National Christian School. He knew Coach Trevor Brown through guys on the DC Assault team, and he got a scholarship and offer to attend this K-12 grade school with 500 students, in Ft. Washington, Maryland. Like Montrose, it was a Christian school with a top basketball program, but they also had a thriving school community beyond basketball, and a good academic program.

Kevin Durant, one of the current top NBA players, was an eighth grader at NCS. He was still developing and didn't play varsity. He ended up playing two years of high school at NCS, then a year at boarding school powerhouse, Oak Hill, then he finished his high school career at Montrose Christian with Stu Vetter. Kevin was on the Blue Devils team with me for several years, although he was not a superstar in those days.

Montrose and NCS played each other in basketball twice each year. I was nervous about going up against my brother, and Coach Vetter knew that.

"Just stay calm, Eric, and focus on your game," he said. I liked that he understood what I was feeling, even though I kept quiet about it.

My mom and my step dad Raymond made up t shirts that had my picture on one side and Earl's on the other. They supported us both and enjoyed the rivalry between our two schools.

It was a heated game, tied 52-52 with 23 seconds left. I went up for a lay-up and my brother fouled me hard. I was mad and in a little bit of pain, but I was able to calm myself down and get to the free throw line. The first one was an easy swoosh. Then I took a deep breath, shot again and scored. It was a small victory for me, and a big one for the team since we won the game 54-52.

Frank Nitti and other guys from my neighborhood came to Montrose to watch my home games. It was always Nitti, and he usually brought Smoke Ears and Mick Moe. They were in their early twenties, and they were powerful people at Sursum Corda. They drove up to Rockville, and I knew they had guns, since they never left the neighborhood unarmed. They loved to follow my game, and I liked hearing them cheer for me on the sidelines. They were supportive of me in every way that they could, both at home and on in the stands.

Coach Vetter said to me, "Eric, your friends are welcome here for our games, but I want you to tell them they have to pull their pants up, and I'd like them to stay in this section of the gym behind my bench."

I was wondering what Nitti and the guys would think of this, but when I told them, they were fine with it. They pulled up their pants a little before coming in and took their spots behind the bench. When Earl and I played each other, they were just as torn as my parents, cheering for both of us.

One night after a game, Coach Vetter came out and introduced himself to the guys. "I appreciate all that you do in keeping Eric safe when he is home," he said. "He and I both appreciate your support in coming here and watching his games."

The guys nodded and talked to Coach Vetter about the game, what they liked, and how glad they were that I was part of such a great basketball program.

"Listen guys," Coach Vetter said to them, "Let me get your shoe sizes and I can see if I have some Nikes in the back for you."

I respected Coach Vetter for this because it showed that he accepted where I came from and who I was. It mattered to me. And it helped solidify Coach Vetter as another person who pulled me along on the right path at that point in my life.

After basketball season, I found myself with free time, which was unusual for me. I got into some trouble one night when I was out with a few Montrose teammates. We were walking around Rockville after midnight with nothing to do and started checking the parked cars to see if there were keys left in the ignition. Soon enough, we found one, and we jumped in to go for a ride. It was thrilling, and exhilarating and I never stopped to think of the consequences.

We rode around, but within fifteen minutes, a

policeman pulled us over. Once I saw those red flashing lights, I thought things were over for me. I got out and kept my hands visible.

"I'm only fifteen," I said, "I don't have a license."

The police officer handcuffed me. I had seen it happen so many times, but when you are actually handcuffed, it is shocking. He took me the station and officially arrested me. It was one in the morning, but they called my mom to come and get me.

She and Raymond drove up to Rockville, and they were angry. My mom said, "I wish they would have kept you for the night to teach you a lesson!"

I was given a court date, but when I went that day, they dropped the charge.

Coach Vetter knew about it and told me sternly, "That was a bad decision. You need to focus on basketball and stop messing around."

It turned out that my days at Montrose were numbered. Coach Vetter had the same policy that Gonzaga did; he wanted students to play in his own summer league.

Coach Vetter was quoted in the Washington Post, explaining why his program had so much turnover. "Kids leave private schools for various reasons," he said, "There are financial and academic considerations as well as location. Rockville can be an hour trip for some of our players. And, of course, kids transfer because of playing time. We have an intense, year-round program and it's not for everybody."

Mike Freeman and Ryan Scott, my best friends on the team, left Montrose to play for public schools. I was getting fatigued from the intense Montrose program. I wanted to take the summer off and play on the AAU circuit, but Coach Vetter would not let me do that.

"I want you here for the summer, working out," Coach Vetter said, "Eric, you need to stay focused."

"I can't come up here to Rockville all summer," I said, "I want to play the summer circuit."

"You have a decision to make, Eric. Stay and play summer basketball with us, or go to another school," he said, "But if you leave, I can guarantee you, you will never go to Duke. It will never happen."

I did leave Montrose Christian, and I never heard from Duke again after that. The letters stopped, and I was completely dropped by their coaching staff. I never knew if they passed over me because of my game, from something Coach Vetter told them about me, or another reason, but my recruiting by Duke ended abruptly after I left Montrose Christian.

Chapter Ten

The summer of 2002 started, and I had no school to go to for tenth grade. It was late June before the word got out that I had left Montrose, and the offers from other schools were not coming in as quickly. Montrose ended up getting two guys from Africa who turned out to be top recruits and went on to have a winning season. I was starting to have doubts about whether leaving Montrose was the right decision.

Stu Vetter had many more good years at the helm, and then resigned from Montrose Christian in 2013. He had spent thirty years as a coach of basketball teams consistently ranked in the top 25 in the country, and he was one of the early leaders of the idea of a national level high school team. In the year of his retirement, he incredibly had 17 players currently on the courts for Division I or NBA teams. Within two years of Coach Vetter's retirement, Montrose Christian School and church closed because of financial problems.

I ended up enrolling in Dunbar High, in Washington, D.C., our local public school. It was overcrowded, underperforming and not exactly what I had envisioned for myself. Earl was heading to Dunbar with me too. He had been kicked out of National Christian for discipline reasons. He was tired of trying new schools and was committed to going to Dunbar and just passing his classes and making it work. I had a different feeling about it. I was disappointed that it had come to this, and I wanted more for myself. From the minute I heard I was going to Dunbar, I tried to seek out ways to find another school.

During the summer tournaments, I had become friends with Luol Deng. Luol was originally from Africa, then moved to London, and was at this point, attending Blair Academy, a boarding school in New Jersey. Luol told me good things about the basketball program and student life at Blair, and I was eager to go there. He talked to his coach, Joe Mantegna, about me.

It turned out that Blair had a formal admissions process with a winter deadline, so there was no way that I could go there for sophomore year. But instead, I made a plan to apply for my eleventh-grade year. I talked with my old tutor Kristin about it, as well as Rob Jackson. Rob talked to Blair's coach Joe Mantegna on my behalf. Kristin spoke to the admissions office and helped me to get registered for the admissions test and to complete the application and essays. In October, just before basketball season started, I took a train to New York, and Kristin met me there and drove me to Blair.

I was in awe of the campus, I had never seen anything like it. It looked more like a college than a high school. They had a dorm with a giant two-story fireplace in the common room, plus an indoor pool, squash courts, basketball courts and work out rooms, a school store, and a stocked cafeteria that was open all day. Considering what Blair offered, what wasn't to like?

I went to my interview dressed in khakis and a shirt and tie, and my enthusiasm was easy to see.

The woman who interviewed me was the Director of Admissions and she told me that she had lived and worked at Blair for almost thirty years.

"How do you think you can contribute to our school community here at Blair?" she asked me.

"I know that you have a great basketball team, so I can contribute to the team and do my best to help them have a winning season," I answered, "But beyond that, I just hope I can be a good member of the community, trying new things and meeting new people. When I was at Holy Trinity School and Gonzaga, I saw how important community is to a school, so I will do my best to add to the community feeling in any way that I can."

She smiled and nodded at me and seemed impressed. It was true, that I had been to schools that had a sense of community and those that didn't, so I was able to articulate what it was about these schools that stood out to me. I hoped that helped me in the interview.

My next stop was the basketball courts where I met Coach Mantegna. He was a young coach who had a lot of enthusiasm and was good at connecting with the players. He asked me a few questions, and I felt like he was really listening to me and trying to get to know me. I saw my friend Luol Deng, and also met Charlie Villanueva and the other guys on the team. I practiced with them and gave it my all since I knew I was being evaluated.

Coach Mantegna was encouraging and said I would be a good fit for the school.

"The acceptance letters for everyone applying to Blair are mailed on March 10. You will have to wait a while to get the official word, but I think you have a good chance of getting in, Eric," he said, "Let's stay in touch this winter."

I always knew I needed someone on my side to help me be successful. At every stage of my life there was someone, in addition to my mom, who helped me get through the year and push me forward. I knew that if there was an adult who believed in me, then it helped me to believe in myself.

This role went unfilled during my year at Dunbar High. There was no coach or teacher there who showed any special interest in me. The school was chaotic and there were so many kids there who had issues and concerns, I suppose that the teachers found it overwhelming. I was able to get straight A's without doing any homework, and I had a lot of free time.

I saw less of Curtis Malone, since his basketball recruiting empire had grown. He had players living in his house, and he was busy with them, and less interested in me. I quit DC Assault and went back to Rob Jackson and the Blue Devils. At this point, I was questioning why I had ever left Rob's team. Curtis did a lot of good for so many guys, and he was kind to me. However, my true connection was with Rob and I wish I had spent more time with him during those years.

Curtis was successful in the coaching world for ten years after I left his team, but then it all ended abruptly. When Curtis Malone's career with DC Assault ended, he was the general manager of a youth basketball program that had 17 teams. He had placed more than one hundred athletes in Division 1 basketball programs and had worked with three top NBA draft picks. He was like the godfather of DC basketball. But Curtis had always been a street guy, and at some point, there was an impetus that made him want to make even more money. He had a tax lien, some financial difficulties, and in 2007, he started selling cocaine again.

For seven years, he ran both DC Assault, the youth basketball program, and a large network for cocaine and heroin distribution. There was a year-long investigation by the IRS, ATF, and DEA, plus state, local and country police. They said that Curtis was smart, covered his tracks, and was difficult to catch. But ultimately, they arrested him in 2012. He was dealing 10,000 kilos of cocaine a month. Court records said that he bought each kilo for $28,000 and sold it for $40,000.

There was shock in the DC area when news got out that Curtis had been arrested. Former players, college coaches, and many other people he had interacted with came to his defense. Well known college coaches like Bob Huggins and Coach K spoke publicly about what good things he had done.

Curtis was complicated. He had changed people's lives. He let young men live with him, he stuck with them when they did wrong, and he pushed them forward and encouraged him. I see him as a good person who got caught up in something he shouldn't have. Others see him as someone who used his players for personal gain.

I was hanging out with Sursum Corda friends a lot more, now that I was at Dunbar High. At night, Sursum Corda was busy and active, I just had to step outside my door and there were groups of people everywhere. One group always hung out at the bottom of the hill, by the grocery store, and another at the top, near the circle, and other kids floated between several groups.

There was a murder in the parking lot in front of my house, related to one person owing another money. A guy was shot and killed. A month later there was a retaliation and another guy was killed. They were people I had known my whole life, only three or four years older than me, but so tightly caught up in the street life that this was the result. Two were dead and two were going to jail.

One night, we were all coming from a "Go Go" party at the infamous High Shop Café. Go Go is a type of music that originated in DC, and it gets its name because the music keeps going, with one song blending into another. It has a reggae base and sampled vocals throughout. I was with my old friend Morris Mitchell, and guys we called Skirt, Rome and Screw Face.

Outside the party, we got into a fist fight with some guys from south of the Anacostia River. Then we walked home and hung out in the parking lot behind Sursum Corda. I noticed a car nearby with people waiting inside.

The car started to move slowly. The window was down, I saw a gun pop out, and my heart raced when I heard shots and realized they were firing at us. It must have been the guys we fought with. They had followed us. Bullets ricocheted off the walls. We all scattered.

The concrete had chipped off the wall right next to where I was standing. I had never felt such fear in my life. We started to run, and I fell and scraped my knee. I saw the blood, and in the confusion, I thought I had been shot.

"I think I've been shot! My leg!" I yelled,

They stopped, and we all realized at the same time, that I was fine, "Keep going! they yelled.

We ran through an alley and it seemed like the car was following us. We jumped over the fence, and I saw the car speed up and drive away.

My adrenaline was pumping, and we had so much energy from our scare. It was the first time I had been shot at. It felt so vivid and real. What a waste if someone had been killed over nothing.

Earl and I were on the same basketball team for the first time ever. We were on the Dunbar varsity, along with Tre Kelly, a guy we knew well from basketball circles. The problem was that all three of us were guards. We were all ball dominated guards who liked to play the point or to shoot a lot. There was a lot of talk about how the three guards with the same style were going to be able to work together on the team and how the ball would be distributed between the three of us. We didn't have any big men for the forward position, so we had to work with the players we had.

I was quoted in the Washington Post commenting that it was our season-long goal to learn to work together effectively, despite what people had been saying about us. Tre took most of the shots, I did a lot of defending, and Earl passed a lot.

It wasn't the best season in terms of team comradery, but we ended up pulling it together by the end. The situation wasn't helped by the fact that our coach was a newbie. Lorenzo Roach had only been coaching for two years, and I don't think he was used to high level basketball. While some of the coaches from my past were weak on basketball technical knowledge, they were strong on motivation and getting guys to work together, or maybe they were good at scouting other teams and getting information. Coach Roach didn't have the skill set or experience for either. He was an extroverted and hyperactive type of coach, who was always giving directions and support from the sidelines.

He meant well and was a good guy, but just didn't have the experience to help us.

It was talent alone that brought us to the public-school city championship in March. We played Cardozo, in a fast-paced game with lots of shooting and scoring. Cardozo had a guy named Roland Williams who scored nine straight three-pointers, including two from well beyond the arch, which wowed the crowds. A more experienced coach would have guided us to get on that guy and shut him down before he got so hot.

The officials at the game were very tough, even calling a violation on one player for having his shirt untucked. Earl had a situation that got him into some trouble. In one moment in the game, he threw the ball in the air out of frustration. It ended up hitting one of the referees who thought it was intentional. Earl got ejected from the game. Despite all this, we did beat Cardozo High and won the public-school title with a 75-62 score.

As public-school champions, our next step was to play the winner of the Washington Catholic Athletic Conference for the City Title. As it turned out, that winner was Gonzaga. It felt sort of awkward and sad to play my old team. I still carried my Gonzaga experience as one of the great positives in my life, and I wasn't looking forward to going up against my old teammates. The three guys who made the team with me freshman year, were all still there; as was Lorenzo Miles, our neighborhood friend who was now a senior.

Despite my good feelings for Gonzaga, I still wanted to beat them. I told Coach Roach about their plays and practice style, but I'm not sure he was able to use any of the information to help us. Gonzaga had never won a City Title, and they were pumped up to win.

Our Dunbar team had one major set-back before the game. Earl was not allowed to play in the game because of his violation of throwing the ball at referee in the last game. Our coach appealed the decision, but ultimately it was considered final and we had to play without him.

The City Title game was played at the George Washington University Smith Center. With a capacity crowd of 5,000 people, it was the largest audience I had ever played for. There was lots of cheering and crowd involvement, and the game had an exciting feel to it. We had a fast style of play, lots of fast breaks and outside shots.

But Gonzaga came out strong and they were the better team that day. They won the City Title, 68-46.

I always hated to lose, and I left the arena with my mom and Raymond, feeling a little blue. When we got home, there was a message on our answering machine that turned things around for me dramatically. It was March 9, and I knew that Blair Academy's decision date was coming up.

My family stood around the answer machine and played the message.

"Eric, it's Coach Mantegna from Blair Academy

calling with good news. You were accepted with a full scholarship. We are looking forward to having you here at Blair! Call me back so we can discuss summer work-outs and your preparation for joining us."

My mom hugged me and said, "Aw, I knew you could do it."

Chapter Eleven

After my season at Dunbar ended, I started playing with the Blue Devils and Rob Jackson, getting ready for the spring and summer tournament season. However, Rob was growing frustrated with me. There was a Blue Devils trip in Texas that I was supposed to go to, but I never showed up at the airport. I am going through a phase where I was feeling very free but less focused. I did what I wanted to do and tried not to think about the consequences. The whole team was there at the airport waiting for the flight to Dallas, and I just never showed up. Rob was furious with me.

I was feeling a little lost, which is what prompted a major decision in my life. I made a commitment to play for John Calipari at the University of Memphis. I didn't talk to anyone about it, I didn't make an official visit, I just did it. I committed. And it turned out to be a decision that caused a lot of drama over the next year.

It all started when I was looking through my giant bin of college recruiting mail. I pulled out one of the brochures from Memphis and looked it over. I liked the idea of Memphis since I knew they sent players to the NBA and ran a solid program. I remembered meeting John Calipari on campus a few years before. I was about 13 or 14 and we had a Blue Devils tournament in Memphis, and we were invited to practice at the gym. Coach Calipari and his assistants came and worked with us. They were impressed with my game and gave me a lot of positive attention and feedback. I remember how Calipari told us that he always looked out for his guys. That stuck in my mind.

I thought to myself, what if I just called him right now and committed? Then I would have him on my side, looking out for me. I would have a spot at a good college. I picked up the phone, dialed the number and waited. Someone answered, and I told him that it was Eric Price, calling for John Calipari. The person said Coach Cal was on the court, but he would give him the message.

I hung up and continued to look through my mail. Two minutes later, the phone rang. My heart was racing, wondering if it could be him.

"This is John Calipari, returning your call."

"Coach Calipari, this is Eric Price."

"Hi, Eric, it's good to hear from you"

"Coach, I wanted to tell you that I want to come and play for you at Memphis. I'm ready to make the commitment."

And just like that, it was done. I felt fantastic. Calipari had just finished a great recruiting class in the year ahead of me. He had Darius Washington and adding me at point guard would be a great combination.

Coach Calipari knew it could be big for the University of Memphis and he was enthusiastic about it.

"Just promise me that you will not de-commit from the program," he said.

I know he takes care of his players and he wants them to have some commitment on their end too. I told him I was serious about it, we talked a bit more, and then hung up. The news was then released to the basketball media.

The NCAA rule was that Memphis could not call me, but I could call them. So even after the commitment, I had to follow the rules about that. I didn't put anything in writing at that time, since I would have to wait until the NCAA Letter of Intent signing period. But since my commitment was in the basketball media and ESPN, and it was noted in the program of all tournaments I played it, it was about as real as it gets.

When I told my mom, she was happy with the decision. Rob found out through the basketball media and was disappointed. He thought that Curtis was involved in this and had brokered some deal or put pressure on me. He wished that I had told him that I was considering a commitment, rather than just going ahead and doing it.

The next sign of trouble was later that week, when Curtis invited me to an event to watch the NBA Championship game. There were a lot of basketball people there, from sneaker company guys, to sports agents, coaches, and prospects, like me. Curtis told an agent from New York that I was headed to Blair Academy to play for Coach Joe Mantegna, and that I had just committed to Memphis and would playing for John Calipari in two years.

Instantly, there was a comment about how the coach from Blair would not be happy with my decision. I didn't know what the reason for this was, but only listened as they had a laugh about it and wished me luck.

Chapter Twelve

arrived at Blair and immediately felt at home. I had already gotten to know the guys on the basketball team through summer practices, so I had that advantage. Everyone was so friendly and proud to be there. We had all been selected through an admissions process with testing, an interview, and writing essays, so Blair was truly a school for achievers of all kinds. I had this immediate sense of wanting to be there and wanting to be a part of it all

I got the feeling that the kids at Blair were all winners who were going places in life. It was such a mix of kids, and I was excited to see that so many of them were international students. I wasn't the only one on scholarship, and we were told that close to 30 percent of the students were on financial aid. But overall, it was an affluent group for sure. It reminded me a lot of Gonzaga or the private schools in Washington, in terms of the type of student who went there.

I moved into my dorm room and hung up my new navy-blue blazer in the closet. I realized that I didn't have any posters, so I decorated my walls with my recruiting letters. Coach Mantegna had a crate of my recruiting mail that had accumulated during the summer, so I hung up the signed letters from the famous coaches, and the brochures and posters with team pictures and mascots.

I met my roommate Tyler, who was a white guy from Pennsylvania who was also a new eleventh grader. We got along great and continued to keep in touch years after our Blair experience.

I was sixteen, living on my own, responsible for my laundry, and managing my own free time. Sursum Corda made me grow up too fast, and so I felt ready for this college type of atmosphere. I always wanted to live away from home since I felt like I didn't have anyone to watch over me, and my old friends were in trouble and it was hard being around that.

The school work was just as hard as it was at Gonzaga. But at Blair we didn't have any help. At Gonzaga, Coach Turner was like our designated parent who was always at the door to make sure we were doing what we should, and helping us with everything, finding us tutors, and getting involved with every aspect of our academic lives. But at Blair, the students were more independent. There was none of that support, not on that level. I had my assignment, I had to do it and if I needed help, I had to ask for it.

I was the type of person who would never do homework in my room at the dorm. I could only do it at a desk in a classroom or library. My dorm was for relaxing. So, I didn't do as much homework as I probably could have. History and English had more reading than I was used to.

One thing I loved about Blair was how great the kids got along. I remember a teacher telling us that our Blair community would probably be the most diverse community any of us would ever live in. We had people from all walks of life and with different personalities and interests. We had students from Africa, South America, Asia, and it didn't matter the color of your skin, everyone was just cool. I had a friend from Saudi Arabia. We had a lot of laughs and he loved having a friend like me who was so different, and I liked having him for a friend for the same reason.

The girls loved my roommate Tyler, who went on to be a model. We got along great and I visited him at his house one weekend. Another guy who was my friend was on the football team and was this big country white guy who used chewing tobacco, which I had never seen. He took me home with him for a weekend to a country town. I was nervous that there were no black people there, but he said I shouldn't worry about that, and I went to a party with him in his town which was near Lehigh University. He was right, everyone was cool, and we had a great time.

Coach Mantegna was a good guy and I liked him a lot. He was coming off an amazing year for his basketball program and was proud of what they had achieved. Blair had just graduated Luol Deng and Charlie Villanueva, who were high school basketball legends.

They were both McDonald's All Americans, top recruits, and overall high-quality people. Luol went to Duke, stayed for only a year before becoming a major NBA draft pick at only 19 years old. Charlie went to UCONN, where he was part of the 2004 NCAA National Championship team, and he stayed for two years before going to the NBA. These guys ended up having major longevity in the game. Luol was still able to sign a $72 million contract with the Lakers in 2016, after he had already played for over ten years. Charlie is on his twelfth year in the NBA and is extensively involved with his foundation and helping others.

Luol and Charlie were models for excellence. Coach Mantegna wanted to continue to have a quality program. There were a lot of bad things going on in in high school and travel team basketball, which included coaches paying players or their families, influencing decisions and pushing players one way or another. Coach Mantegna and Blair had avoided all that and wanted to continue to run a high-quality program.

When I told Coach Mantegna that I was going to play for John Calipari at the University of Memphis, he was not happy about it. At that time, people thought that John Calipari was slippery, dishonest, and on the bad side of basketball. He was brash and controversial. People in the basketball world, including legendary coach Bobby Knight, went on the record saying bad things about him.

Coach Calipari's first head coaching job was at

UMASS, a struggling basketball program, but he turned it around and brought them to the Final Four. But then it turned out that Marcus Camby, the star player, had taken money from agents, so the team was stripped of its win. People thought Coach Calipari had something to do with that, even though I really don't think he did.

By 2007, Memphis was the number one ranked team in the AP poll and Coach Calipari led them to the Final Four. But this was 2003, when I committed, and Coach Mantegna, and many others, didn't see what was coming for John Calipari. They only saw a guy who went against the grain and left a tarnished UMASS program. For these reasons, Coach Mantegna questioned why I would want to go there.

He pulled me into his office on one of my first days at Blair and said, "Eric, you are a good player with a lot of potential and you are only a junior. You have time to open up your search."

I said, "I know what I want to do, I want to play for Coach Calipari."

Coach Mantegna told me that Coach Calipari does things the wrong way, and that people question his integrity. He encouraged me to de-commit from Memphis. He said that college coaches would be coming to Blair during the season and I would get exposure to lots of programs. "I always take care of my players, and I will take you of you. Committing to Memphis was the wrong decision."

Now I had a dilemma. I had to play for this high school coach who I admired, who was questioning my decision. I was in a difficult spot and was unsure of what to do.

I waited almost two months before I did what Coach Mantegna suggested. By then, I was so immersed in Blair life and as part of the Blair basketball team that it seemed like the right thing to do. Coach Mantegna was now that mentor or influencer that I always needed in my life, so I listened to him. Before the basketball season started in November, I called Memphis and de-committed. Just as I had so quickly become a Memphis Tiger with one phone call, now one phone call erased all that.

I was the starting point guard on the Blair team and I benefitted from good coaching and team unity. We didn't travel a lot, but we played St. Anthony's from Jersey City, and St. Patrick from Elizabeth, which were perennial nationally ranked powerhouses. We played another boarding school in New Jersey called Lawrenceville, which is an elite college prep school with a beautiful campus.

At that time, Lawrenceville had Joakim Noah, who became an NBA standout. He was well known even then, since he was a top recruit and his father is Yannick Noah, the French tennis legend. We had a fight on the court, and even now, when I watch Joakim on tv, I just don't like the guy.

The fight spread into the stands and involved my

mom. We were at the Lawrenceville campus, and the stands were packed. My mom and my stepdad Raymond drove up from Washington with my aunt Shinny. I could hear them in the stands, cheering for me.

I went in for a layup and I missed it and Joakim fouled me hard. He is known for that. He is a tough player. My mom yelled, and both Joakim and I looked over at her in the stands and she said, "You foul my son again like that, I'm coming on the court after you!"

Then Joakim's mom stood up, and then my aunt got up, and they were screaming at each other in the stands. Then it turned to pushing and everyone was looking at them. Eventually some staff members broke it up and asked them all to leave.

We ended up finishing the game, and we were fine, although Joakim and I talked a lot of trash. My mom wasn't scared during the incident at all, she was very protective of me. She was usually the only voice I could hear on the court since she was so loud and always so supportive. "Control your attitude, Toe!" she would say to me, or "Control it, before you get a tech!" Her words really helped me to stay focused and in control.

Something very bad happened back home while I was at Blair. My first reaction when I heard about it was relief that I wasn't there. But the problem with getting one foot out the door of the projects is that it always finds a way to whip you right back to where you came from. When I first heard the news that a child was murdered two doors down from my house, I never would have guessed that things would transpire in a way that would soon end my career at Blair.

There was a girl at Sursum Corda named Jahkema Princess Hansen, but she went by her middle name and it suited her in a lot of ways. Princess was a force at Sursum Corda, rolling with high powered people in the neighborhood, doing things that I would have never dared to try when I was her age. She was a seventh grader and had just turned 14 on Christmas day. She was dating one of the big drug dealers in the area, a 28-year-old named Marquette Ward. I know that may be shocking, but that was the truth.

There were two murders at Sursum Corda on a cold Saturday night in January. Princess witnessed one of them which is where all the trouble started. Princess and Marquette were out at 3am that night together. One version of the story says that they were attempting to buy a PCP laced cigarette from a small-time drug dealer named Mario Evans. Marquette wanted a discount, Evans insisted on full-price, and Marquette shot him in the head. Other versions say that Mario was working for Marquette and they had a dispute over business. Whatever the reason, Marquette killed Mario, and Princess witnessed it, along with a young woman named Tamika Holiday.

Now, I know that Princess is no snitch. I had known her my whole life. She never would have told. But somehow, things unfolded in an unusual way, and there was suspicion that Princess might snitch after all. People could see that the police were at her house. Marquette was concerned.

The details of the story came out eventually in the press and in court documents, and through talk around Sursum Corda. Princess and her mother, Judyann Hansen, went to the police station to talk to the officers. And make note that Princess didn't go in there as a shy seventh grader, she went in with swagger.

"Why would I snitch?" she asked the police detectives, defiantly.

Her mother piped in that maybe the police would provide them with protection or move them out of Sursum Corda. But Princess pointed out that her two older brothers were in the DC prison system and snitching would make their life even more difficult on the inside.

Police detective Willie Jefferson offered Princess protection and warned her of the danger she faced, saying that a gunman will "come and put you to sleep because he don't want to do 60 years."

At Marquette's trial for murder, Jefferson testified that Princess told him that she "was not there at the shooting," that she knew nothing about it, that she "wasn't no snitch," and that nothing was going to happen to her because she had she was dating Marquette Ward.

Princess left the police station that day, feeling confident. No deal. No stitching. She had been in touch with Marquette who told her to "lay low" and promised her some money for staying quiet.

That night, Judyann Hansen went out to the clubs, and encouraged her daughter to stay inside for the night. Princess agreed to stay home, saying that it was too cold of a night to go out.

But Princess did, in fact, go out. She went to the Sursum Corda home of Timika Holiday, the 20-year-old who was also there that night when Marquette shot Mario Evans. Timika used sex for power, calling it in court, not prostitution, but "even exchange." Princess and Timika were waiting for Marquette to send someone over with their hush money. Also in the house was 12-year-old Tonique White, Timika's sister.

Marquette got his man, Frank Nitti, the neighborhood enforcer and my older friend and protector, to do the job for him. But rather than asking Nitti to deliver cash, he paid him $8,000 to kill Princess. Nitti burst through the door, shooting young Tonique in the leg. Princess started to run through the small house and Nitti chased her, shooting her twice in the back of the head, killing her instantly.

The death of a 14-year-old witness, and all the sordid details that went along with it, made for a big news story. It wasn't just the Washington Post, but also the syndicated papers picked up the story, so it was all over the country. It was mentioned on national news shows and morning shows, here and internationally. People wondered how something so vile could happen less than a mile from the US Capitol. There was discussion of who to blame—the DC police, the housing authority, the mayor—and what action could be taken to keep this from happening again.

The news made it to Blair Academy. I don't remember how it first came up, but some of the teachers made the connection that I was from Sursum Corda. And one teacher had the idea that I should share my experiences with the whole school. At Blair, we had Chapel Talks, where a member of the school community spoke during chapel about something that he overcame, a challenge he faced, or just any moment related to personal development.

I don't remember which teacher suggested it to me, but I know that she told me that I should do a Chapel Talk on the Sursum Corda murders. She told me that Blair kids come from privileged backgrounds and I should share my story with them. It will help them to open their eyes, to be humbler, and to understand how others live.

To my 17-year-old self, this seemed like a good idea. It was an honor to give a Chapel Talk. An adult who I respected felt that I had something I could share with others, something that would be well received and may be a way to make a little bit of good out of a bad situation. So, I agreed to do it. I spent quite a while writing my talk. I wish that I still had it, so I could recount exactly what I said that night, but I don't.

I walked up to the podium in the big chapel and looked out at all the silent faces of the students and faculty of Blair Academy. I never got nervous in basketball games with these same people watching me, but this time, it was different. It felt like a big moment of awkward silence when I unfolded my paper and began to talk.

I told them about Sursum Corda, some of the things I witnessed, and what life was like there. I told them about Princess, who I had known most of my life, and about Nitti, who had protected me and cheered me on throughout my childhood. I told them that people are complicated, everything isn't so black and white as you think. People in poor neighborhoods with few opportunities do things that those of us in better circumstances could never imagine doing. It doesn't excuse it, but it might help those who are trying to figure out how these things happen.

After the Chapel Talk, I immediately noticed that there was a change in how people perceived me. Some girls dropped off sympathy cards under my dorm room door. A few guys offered to help me out, buy me anything that I needed. Other people avoided me. It made me feel awkward, uncomfortable, and eventually, devastated. This wasn't what I had intended. I didn't want anyone feeling sorry for me. I didn't want anyone judging me because of where I came from. But it seemed like that was exactly what was happening.

Before my talk, no one at Blair had known I was from a rough neighborhood. Remember, I started private school in Georgetown when I was 10 and I had traveled extensively, three or four airplane trips per year, throughout my childhood. Those experiences and that exposure to people effected how I presented myself. I was well spoken, well dressed, I never gave anyone any sign whatsoever that I had lived that way. No one knew unless I told them, and I told very few people. I think that Blair kids assumed I came from an affluent family.

And so now, everyone knew. And it wasn't good. I am not the type of guy who wants anyone to feel sorry for me. How people treated me after the talk was a shock to me and it effected my status at Blair. I even felt that some teachers started to back away from me. I had been a part of this amazing community of students from around the world, and now that was over, and I was on the outside.

At this point, basketball season had ended, so I lost that anchor. I was supposed to play a spring sport, and I agreed to run track, but I rarely went to the practices. I needed to work on my grades, visit my teachers more often for extra help, but I didn't do that either. I felt that things were a little strained between me and Coach Mantegna. My college recruiting was still active, but it had slowed, and I was beginning to regret decommitting from University of Memphis.

I have always said that I can't be successful on my own. And as spring came at Blair Academy, I was feeling increasingly alone. That snowballed for me. I felt that people were pulling away from me, so I pulled away more. Now there was a gulf between us.

One night in late April, I decided to sneak out at night to see this beautiful Asian girl named Nicole who I really liked. Kids at Blair did break rules from time to time, and usually no one found out. But this time, someone snitched on me. As soon as I left the dorm, a boy I knew told the house parent, and I was caught. I was expelled from Blair that night. It wasn't just about sneaking out, I had also failed to attend several commitments during the school days, and it was obvious that I wasn't a part of the Blair community anymore.

My mom drove up to New Jersey the next day to pick me up. She felt sorry for me but assured me that everything would be ok. I went back to Dunbar High School the very next day, to register again and finish out the last seven weeks of my junior year.

Chapter Thirteen

I was worn out from picking new schools and starting over. I had already been to four high schools and still had a year to go. People are critical of young athletes who change schools so often, and I was afraid that the colleges might be concerned with the fact that I was a serial school-changer.

In the long run, my experience was actually a positive thing for me. I met so many different types of people, I learned to play for coaches with different styles, and I adapted to change. There are not many other people in this world who have attended an all boys' Jesuit high school, a prestigious boarding school, a small Christian academy, and an inner-city public school. I value all those experiences and I learned from the people who I met there. I hoped the colleges would look at it this way too.

But at the time that I returned to Dunbar in April of my junior year, I was not feeling so positive about things. I felt bad about it. I had been proud to leave and make it to Blair, and it was humbling to come back. People had a lot of questions and there was a lot of talk. I realized that basketball had taken me so many places, yet it seemed out of my control. The shootings at Sursum Corda had shaken me. I started to think less about basketball and more about my own survival.

Going back to Dunbar was stressful. There was a period for several months where I worried about where I would end up in life. I was looking for both a college and a high school to go to and it was overwhelming. I started to spend more time with my friends in Sursum Corda. I wanted a break from basketball. This was the time I should have been focused on making the most of the summer tournament season, but instead I just wanted a break from my life.

I went to a few of the Blue Devils tournaments with Rob, but I skipped just as many. I attended the USA Basketball Youth Development Festival in Colorado, because it was a high-level showcase and I was honored to get an invitation. But it was difficult to focus on my game when I had so much going on in my life.

I missed a Blue Devils tournament in New Orleans where Ty Lawson, Kevin Durant and our other teammates played a tough Georgia Stars team. Rob was quoted in the local press saying, "Eric Price has been playing outstanding basketball for us in practices. He has been looking great. I think that if Eric had been with us, we would have beaten the Georgia Stars." Rob knew I was going through a difficult time, and he spoke to the press in this positive way about me, which was one thing that helped me to move forward at a tough time.

By the end of the summer, I realized that I had to pick a high school. The biggest early contender for my fifth high school was Hargrave Military Academy. This all boys' school in rural Virginia had developed a pipeline to Division 1 basketball programs. The basketball players had to fully participate in military life, which was unappealing to me. When Rob Jackson spoke with me about it, I didn't like much of what I heard.

My friend Isaiah Swann ended up going to Hargrave. He told me this story about how they had an important away game and they were supposed to meet at the bus at 2pm. Isaiah was busy getting his things together and when he arrived at the gym five minutes after two, he wondered where everyone was. Eventually he realized the bus had left without him. Hargrave was big on life lessons and instilling a sense of discipline, routine, and order. The guy who I was at seventeen-years-old would have benefitted from that tremendously, but I was also not the type to choose that path for myself. I couldn't see myself at a military school. I had led an independent life since I was young, mostly making my own decisions, and I didn't want to go into an environment that was so rigid.

Rob Jackson encouraged me to give it a try. He told me that Billy Donovan from the University of Florida offered me a spot on his team if I would go to Hargrave and prove I could be successful there. The offer was alluring, but ultimately, I said no. I thought I didn't need a place like Hargrave. Looking back, it probably would have helped me a lot, but at that time, I didn't see it.

I ended up taking a different path and enrolling in a basketball focused school called Coastal Christian Academy. I heard about it through the coach, Walter Webb, a guy I knew from DC basketball circles. Walter was in his early thirties and was bright and ambitious. He had played professionally in China and ran a basketball business called Slam City, which sponsored AAU teams and had good success with some older post graduate players who hadn't signed with a college yet.

Walter was honest and straight-forward. "Our team is going to play a national schedule of more than thirty games a season. I can get you out there in front of colleges, competing at a higher level."

It sounded good to me, so I moved down to Virginia to start my senior year. Coastal Christian Academy was only a church with a preschool. The addition of the prep basketball program two years before I arrived was their introduction into the high school world. There were only eleven students in the high school, and we were all on the basketball team. We were all seniors or post graduates. I lived with five other guys in a house that Walter Webb rented for us.

Coastal Christian did not have teachers or classes, so we followed an on-line curriculum. I was able to do my work at my own pace. I didn't worry about whether I was learning enough because I was focused on basketball. I liked the independent learning, even though it was a very different way of life

Walter was a talented coach and he ran a solid basketball program. We had a team that included several guys who had already committed to top Division 1 programs but needed time to get their grades and testing up to qualify for NCAA requirements. Leo Criswell, a 6-9 forward who went on to Mizzou was our top player, and we also had three other big forwards over six foot seven who had come from Africa, and several fast and skilled guards.

When I was in Virginia finishing my last year of high school, my brother Earl had moved to California and was playing basketball at a junior college. He ended up staying in California for more than ten years, and I didn't see him much during this time.

Earl's journey in high school took him to Laurinburg Institute, a historically black boarding school in North Carolina that had a top basketball program. But he had a lot on his mind. His girlfriend was expecting a baby. He had been involved in the street life in Sursum Corda, had some situations that really weighed on his mind. He left Laurinburg and went back to Dunbar to graduate.

Earl did not qualify academically for a Division 1 scholarship, so he accepted one of the many offers he received from junior colleges. Because of problems that he had in the neighborhood, he realized that going to California and creating some distance between himself and the street life was his best option.

I enjoyed my time at Coastal Christian and was starting to get motivated about basketball again. Coach Webb was a well-liked coach who attracted talent. He knew how to manage and motivate a team. He had a good system and plan for me and I was averaging twenty-three points a game, which was the best I had ever done.

The SAT test is a big part of the process of getting a college scholarship. I had been to high school for five years, so I had fulfilled the course requirements and had the grades that I needed. But the SAT was a different story. I had changed schools so often, that I never got good advice about it. It ended up presenting a big problem for me.

I was registered to take the SAT during my junior year at Blair. But I got kicked out in April, a few weeks before I was supposed to take the test. I should have arranged to take the test at home in Washington. But I was so consumed with my problems at that time, that I didn't even think about the SAT, or trying to figure out how to contact them and make the change. It wasn't on my radar.

Coastal Carolina didn't have a guidance counselor or teachers, so my advice was fragmented. I heard from some people that I needed to hire someone to take the SAT for me. I heard from others that I had to study for it, but I didn't know how I would do that. Our team was on the road a lot and no one else seemed to be worrying about the SAT.

Finally, one weekend when I was home in Washington, I took the SAT. My mother got up to cook me some breakfast. I had been out the night before with friends and went into the test feeling a little tired and looking at this difficult test that I had not reviewed for. After I took it, I went back to Coastal Christian and didn't give it much more thought.

After basketball season ended in March, I spent most of my time staying with friends at North Carolina A&T University. Ronnie Webb, who I met at Gonzaga and who became a lifelong friend of mine, was a student there. Since there was nothing going on at Coastal Christian after basketball season ended, I spent most of my time there hanging out. Even my recruiting mail was coming to Ronnie's address. Since I had a good season at Coastal Christian, there were still college coaches who were contacting me.

The coaching staff from Wake Forest was interested in me. They sent a limo to pick me at North Carolina A&T and bring me to campus for a work out. Ronnie and I both got out of the limo and were surprised to see students and staff members welcome us at the car, carrying giant Wake Forest umbrellas. We had a tour of the campus, and then met the basketball staff. They had an open gym for me and watched me work out with their team.

Things must have gone well since they offered me a scholarship that day. They suggested that I start immediately and register for summer school classes. I was ready to accept.

A staff member started the process of gathering my transcripts and registering me with the NCAA Clearinghouse. I needed to qualify academically in order to be eligible to accept the offer. I didn't have the SAT results, even though I had taken the test months ago. Maybe they mailed it to my mother's house, but I never got it.

I called my old tutor Kristin and asked her how I could find out what my SAT score was. She found the number, and we were both on the line, calling the College Board and asking them to look up my SAT score. The lady on the phone seemed to be so sad to tell me the news. My score was too low.

I didn't qualify under NCAA regulations and I could not accept the offer from Wake Forest.

Epilogue

Whatever happened to Eric Price? That is a question I have seen on basketball blogs over the years. And sometimes I hear it in person, when I run into people I knew from basketball circles who wondered how my journey and my story ended. I want to tell everyone that my life continued to move forward after basketball. As a wise Gonzaga teacher told me long ago, you can't let basketball consume you. And I didn't. I also didn't let the fact that I never played in the NBA consume me or get me down.

After realizing that I didn't qualify academically to accept my offer from Wake Forest, I quickly moved on to the next option, which was junior college. I had plenty of offers there, all full scholarships.

I went to Chipola Junior College in Marianna, Florida. I majored in English and helped lead the Indians to a 33-3 record and a trip to the championship game of the NJCAA tournament. I played in all 36 games and led the team in scoring.

I moved on to Blinn Junior College in Texas, where I played in nine games before getting a rib injury that ended my season. Ready to move on to a bachelor's degree program, I evaluated several colleges, and accepted a full scholarship from Fort Lewis College in Colorado.

My basketball career brought me to five high schools and three colleges, and I learned something from every coach and experience I had. I became extremely adaptable and I never gave up. I had set-backs, yet I always found the strength to keep going. I didn't dwell on disappointment or worry about what others said. It was not easy to see guys who I played with, guys who I dominated, making millions in the NBA. But what I had been through made me strong enough to get past this, and to keep moving forward with my life just as I did when I was a boy.

My childhood as a young basketball player helped me to escape the fate that so many of my friends from Sursum Corda faced. Basketball opened doors for me. It took me places that I literally never would have had the opportunity to go. I truly believe seeing is believing. Basketball showed me that there is more out there.

I used basketball, I did not allow it to use me. I learned from basketball that how you handle failure is just as important how you handle success. I finished school with no debt. I became a teacher, working at first as an aide, then I had my own grade school class, and eventually I was teaching high school math.

I met my wife, Yahne Price, at North Carolina A&T, introduced by my best friend Ronnie. She is a nurse, and together we purchased a home in Maryland in 2015 and married soon after. We are expecting our first child, a son, in April of 2019. Yahne and I have traveled the world together, including Dubai, Paris, Barcelona, Venice, Madrid, Thailand, Turks and Caicos, and Hawaii. I feel so alive when I travel. It was basketball that introduced me to travel, and it will always be a passion of mine.

I have always tried to be more. Love more. Create peace. Even when people try to tear you down.

For people who ask, "What ever happened to Eric Price?" I'd say, here I am. I grew up to be a family man with integrity who is committed to making the world a better place.

About the Author

Eric Price is an elementary school teacher in Washington, DC. He coaches boys' travel basketball with Team Takeover and is a speaker for youth groups and schools on the topic of resilience.

Eric was a nationally ranked basketball player during his youth, playing at select tournaments and showcases throughout the country. Today, Eric and his wife, Yahne, live in Upper Marlboro, Maryland. This is his first book.

Eric can be reached at priceeric2003@gmail.com.

Made in the USA
Middletown, DE
25 March 2019